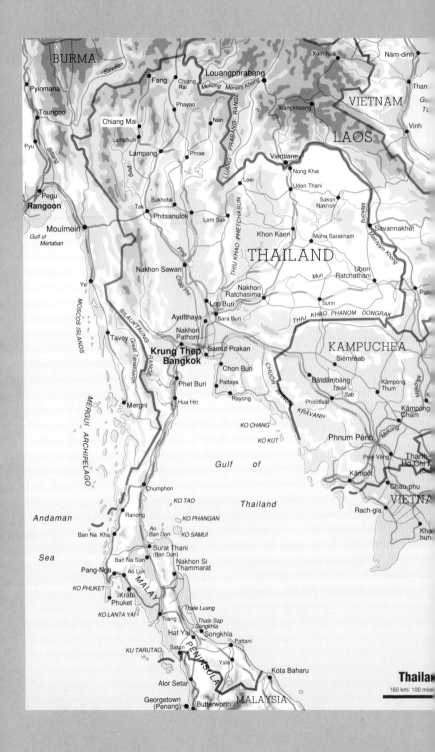

INSIGHT *pocket* GUIDES

CHIANG MAI

ใบเสียงทา
ของ

Written and Presented by **Steve Van Beek**

INSIGHT *pocket* GUIDES

Insight Pocket Guide:

CHIANG MAI

Directed by
Hans Höfer

Photography by
Steve Van Beek

Design Concept by
V. Barl

Design by
Karen Hoisington

© 1994 APA Publications (HK) Ltd

All Rights Reserved

Printed in Singapore by
Höfer Press (Pte) Ltd
Fax: 65-8616438

Distributed in the United States by
Houghton Mifflin Company
222 Berkeley Street
Boston, Massachusetts 02116-3764
ISBN: 0-395-69017-X

Distributed in Canada by
Thomas Allen & Son
390 Steelcase Road East
Markham, Ontario L3R 1G2
ISBN: 0-395-69017-X

Distributed in the UK & Ireland by
GeoCenter International UK Ltd
The Viables Center, Harrow Way
Basingstoke, Hampshire RG22 4BJ
ISBN: 9-62421-507-3

Worldwide distribution enquiries:
Höfer Communications Pte Ltd
38 Joo Koon Road
Singapore 2262
ISBN: 9-62421-507-3

Sawasdee!

Steve Van Beek

I had not been in Thailand more than a week when a Thai friend said, 'If you want to see Thailand at its most beautiful, go to Chiang Mai.' This, and Chiang Mai's reputation for having the most beautiful women in Thailand propelled me towards the train station.

In a third class car on a day train to Chiang Mai, I got my first glimpse of the broad valley of the Chao Phya River. It was the middle of the monsoon season but the dampness only enhanced the brilliant green of the rice fields. The Thais around me were not letting the grey weather dampen their spirits. They laughed, joked and handed me sections of oranges and magic coconut milk sweets that melted in my mouth. In the process, they introduced me not only to the beauty of the countryside but of the people as well.

When, at last, the train chugged into Chiang Mai Station, I had a half-dozen invitations to stay at their homes as an honoured guest. I wrote down all the addresses but, in the end, went off in search of my own Chiang Mai.

During this visit, a number of sights stirred my blood: Doi Suthep, Wat Phra Singh and Wat Chedi Luang in particular stand out. The northern women were lovely but their beauty was a natural extension of their surroundings. When I boarded the train for Bangkok, I vowed I would return. And I have, time and again.

But it is to a different Chiang Mai each time. The town, 20 years later, is caught up in a frenzy of construction. Yet, the Chiang Mai I remember is still here. It lives in the backstreets, the temples, the lovely Ping River, and in nearby towns and fields of the valley: Doi Suthep still sparkles from its hilltop redoubt and the women are as beautiful as ever.

You are about to discover some of the most beautiful art in Asia, some of the most striking scenery and a people who, despite rapid development, are still friendly and willing to help strangers and foreigners alike. So, let's get started.

As the sign at the exit of Wat Jet Yot says: 'Have a nice trip to you'. *Sawasdee – Welcome!*

Contents

*Preceding pages: hilltribe village
in Doi Thong, Chiang Rai*

Following pages: Meo hilltribe children

Lanna, land of a million rice fields, is the name by which the North and its culture have been known for centuries. Bordered by the Mekong River and the mountains of Burma and walled off by jungle from the Central Plains, Lanna lived in remote splendour until early this century. It had its own royal families, spoke its own dialect, and fought its own battles with Burmese and Siamese armies.

The early power bases were along the Mekong River. In the mid-13th century, King Mengrai marched south to create an empire in Kok River Valley, establishing the city of Chiang Rai in 1262. After capturing Haripunchai (Lamphun) and securing joint leadership of Phayao, he sought a more central headquarters and looked for one in the Ping River Valley.

He constructed a palace/fortress at Wiang Kung Kam (its remains are just south of the Superhighway) and a temple, Chedi Liem, but they were unsuitable so he moved just north to establish Chiang Mai (New City) in 1296. Because the Ping River frequently overflowed its banks, he built his royal city on high ground to the west, surrounding it with a brick and earth wall 1.6 km (1 mile) on a side; and surrounded by a defensive moat. A smaller wall, remnants of which still exist along Kamphaeng Din Road, once embraced a residential section.

The flowering of Lanna culture dates from the reign of warrior king Tilokaraja. So influential was he that the 8th World Buddhist Council was held in Chiang Mai in 1455. Less than a century later, however, the kingdom was embroiled in internecine disputes that weakened it, a situation the Burmese were not slow to exploit. After repeated battles, it fell to the King of Pegu in 1558 and was ruled by the Burmese for the next two centuries.

While Burma spared Chiang Mai, the destruction that it visited upon Ayutthaya in 1767 was devastating. It conscripted its young men and expropriated supplies for its war against Laos. So severe did the hardships become that, like several other cities of the North including Chiang Rai, Chiang Saen, Sukhothai, and Phayao, its inhabitants simply abandoned the town of Chiang Mai. It remained empty for 20 years until a Chiang Mai hero, Prince Kawila, triumphed over the Burmese in 1799 and established his headquarters in the city.

Culture

Prince Kawila, hero of Chiang Mai

For most of the 19th century, Chiang Mai was ignored by both Burma and Siam. It was not until the European colonial powers (the British in Burma and the French in Laos) began casting covetous eyes at the region that Bangkok's rulers realised their sovereignty over the area was in danger. In 1877, a Thai Viceroy took up residence in Chiang Mai although, until 1939, he ruled through a Chiang Mai prince.

The North acquired new importance with the dawn of the 20th century. A railway, begun in 1898, was pushed north through jungle and formidable mountains, the last rail being laid in 1921. The railway eliminated the tortuous journey up the Chao Phya and Ping Rivers that took six weeks or more.

The thickly-forested hills drew the attention of foreign teak merchants who bought concessions and began floating logs down the rivers to Bangkok. When the concessions lapsed, the Forest Industry Organization took over and have since played a part in denuding much of the forested northern hills.

While cities to the south began to grow as a result of investment by the U.S. government in support of the Indochina war, Chiang Mai remained stable. The last fifteen years, however, have seen some dramatic changes. Farming is being modernised and in the southern valley, industrial plants are replacing rice seedlings. The city is experiencing rapid growth as condominiums and hotels mushroom high above the skyline. Once-empty spaces are rapidly being filled with housing estates.

Yet, there are still pockets of the past in the back streets. And once the visitor steps outside the valley, he discovers a different pace of life, more like that which drew him here in the first place.

Aerial view of Chiang Mai from the top of Pornping Hotel

Geography

Thailand is generally divided into four regions, each of them capitalized, eg., North, as in North, South, East, and West. The 'North' refers to the entire northern region which surrounds Chiang Mai. Non-capitalized 'north' refers to directions, for eg., 'northeast'.

Chiang Mai is the political and geographic capital of the North by virtue of its central position and size. As Thailand's second largest city, it is home to some 170,000 people and dominates the economic and social life of the Chiang Mai Valley. Outside the valley wall are five key regions of the North. To the west is the area comprising the valleys of Mae Chaem, Pai, Mae Hong Son and Mae Sarieng.

Beyond the Khun Tan range of mountains to the south is Lampang. The third area, to the east, encompasses cities like Phayao and Ngao. In the green valleys north of Chiang Mai are Chiang Dao and Fang.

The fifth region is dominated by Chiang Rai. It is defined in the north and west by the Mekong River, an area known as the Golden Triangle for the three countries that border it and for its association with opium cultivation. Towns here include Mae Sai, Chiang Saen and Chiang Khong.

The People and Hilltribes

Lanna Thais speak a dialect quite distinct from that of the Central Plains. They are almost exclusively Theravada Buddhists although there are Mahayana Buddhists, Muslims and Sikhs in the larger towns. Of all the regions in Thailand where Christian missionaries strove to win converts, they were most successful in the North, as the many churches attest. They also had considerable influence among the hilltribes, primarily the Lahus and the Karens.

Lanna Thais are primarily lowland rice farmers, laboriously engineering the land into paddies in which they plant two crops of rice each year. Unlike Chinese villages inhabited by a single clan, Thai villages contain many families unrelated to each other. Yet at planting and harvest time, they pool their labour for mutual benefit. The village is a democratic unit presided over by a *phu yai baan* (headman) or a *kamnan* (head of a group of villages) although he (there are a few headwomen as well) generally comes from the wealthiest family in the village.

The Buddhist *wat* (temple) formerly anchored the village. Temple buildings served as meeting halls, the murals on the interior walls were illustrated instruction books on religion and the arts, and monks were the teachers, herbal doctors, and arbitrators in village disputes. Today, many of their roles have been taken over by government

The chedi of Wat Doi Suthep

agencies but they continue to wield considerable influence.

In addition to the Thai peoples of Lanna, there are major racial groups like the Thai Yai and Shans whose culture and languages are similar. If theories are correct, most of these people originated in China and migrated south over 10 centuries ago. More recent arrivals include the Chinese and the hilltribes.

For most visitors, the hilltribes are the North's most colourful inhabitants. Each of the six principal groupings – Hmong (Meo), Lisu, Akha, Lahu (Musur), Yao and Karen – have a distinct language incomprehensible to the others. With ancient origins in China, they arrived in Thailand's northern hills in recent centuries. Despite their differences, there is little conflict between them. No group claims a particular area as its own and villages intermingle and overlap throughout the North, primarily along the borders with Burma.

These major tribal groupings are sub-divided according to the colours – Blue, White, or Red – of the costumes they wear. Each has its own patterns and styles of clothing. There are also lesser tribes like the elusive Phi Thong Luang (Spirits of the Yellow Leaves), Lua, H-tin, Khamu, Wa.

Meo hilltribe women

Rice seedlings

As nomadic farmers, the hill-tribes practice a slash-and-burn or 'swidden' form of agriculture. They cut down a tract of forest and burn off the undergrowth to plant a crop. A few years later, when the soil's fertility has been depleted by the crop, the hill-tribe move onto other virgin areas to begin the whole cultivation process all over again.

Population pressures, a shortage of land, and government programmes to encourage them to settle in particular areas, have reduced the tribes' nomadic instincts considerably. The government has also been largely successful in luring four of the tribes – Hmong, Yao, Akha, and Lisu – away from cultivation of opium. The crop has created a crime problem in the area known to the world as the Golden Triangle where warlords operate illegal caravans and laboratories to process the poppy into heroin, in open defiance of the Thai government.

Projects initiated by His Majesty in the 1970s provide seed and assistance to grow and market more socially acceptable crops. The northern hills have proven themselves to be as adaptable as the hill-tribes, nourishing such diverse crops as asparagus, mushrooms,

strawberries, apples and coffee.

The hilltribe culture, however, has revealed itself to be fragile under the onslaught of alien values brought by the Thais and the intrusion in recent years by tourists. The former have attempted to incorporate the hilltribes into the mainstream, more for chauvinistic reasons than in consideration of their needs, and the toll has been heavy. Tourists were initially drawn by the unique cultures the tribes represented but their sheer numbers are threatening to overwhelm the tiny villages, creating an unhealthy dependence on outsiders.

New cabbages

These are the populations, areas of habitation, and characteristics of the six principal hilltribes:

Karen: At an estimated 300,000, the Karens are the largest hilltribe in Thailand but are minor by comparison with the nearly five million in neighbouring Burma. They are thought to have originated in Tibet more than 2,600 years ago and have lived here for 200 years. They are concentrated west of Chiang Mai, northwest of Chiang Rai, and along the border to Phetchaburi.

Hmong (Meo): The best-known of the hilltribes, their 70,000 members live near the Laotian border, north and east of Chiang Mai. There are also a few south of Tak.

Yao: The Yao seem to have migrated from southern China about two centuries ago. While 1.3 million live in China and 200,000 in Vietnam, there are only 20,000 in Thailand, most of them around Chiang Rai, Nan, and near the Laotian border.

Lahu (Musur): Originating in Yunnan, China, they migrated into Thailand via eastern Burma in the last century. Now numbering 55,000, their villages are

Hilltribe home

Lisu children

along the Burmese border, north of Chiang Mai and near Chiang Rai.

Akha: The so-called 'dog eaters', for their culinary preferences, originated south of Kunming in China's Yunnan province and began moving south about the turn of the century. They total 28,000 and live primarily north of Chiang Mai and Chiang Rai.

Lisu: Thought to have originated in eastern Tibet, they are the latest arrivals, the first recorded tribesmen having settled here in 1921. Now numbering 24,000, they live near the Burmese border north of Chiang Mai and west of Chiang Rai.

Northern Culture

Although flavoured by contact with Burma and Laos, Lanna culture is unique. In addition to special dishes found only in the North, Lanna temple architecture is immediately recognizable.

As the temple is built on a low base of stucco-covered brick, a northern temple seems squat in contrast to the soaring temples of the Central Plains. Its roofs rise in three tiers from low, generally windowless, walls, sweeping in flat, graceful curves like the wings of gigantic birds.

The bounty of northern teak forests has also allowed extensive use of wood both to clad the building and to provide deeply-carved decorations along its gable. The *viharn* (sermon hall) has a front portico supported by four columns. The upper sections of the spaces between the columns are curved like eyebrows, said to be a symbolic representation of hidden eyes watching over the populace.

The interior is generally plain. Representative of Lanna structures is kingpost construction to support the roof. The ceiling is also decorated with gold lotuses and stars on a red background. In newer temple buildings, there is a strong preference for gold and bright red, often to the point of garishness.

There are a variety of *chedi* (stupa) styles including the square pyramid of the early Haripunchai period (Wat Kukut in Lamphun and Wat Chedi Liem in Chiang Mai), square pyramids with dented corners (Chiang Mai's Wat Chedi Luang and Wat Doi Suthep), the later Haripunchai style with its compact base and tall spire (Lamphun's Wat Phra That Haripunchai), and circular chedis punctuated with niches holding standing Buddha images (Chiang Mai's Wat Rampoeng).

The visitor to Chiang Mai has ample opportunity to study such monuments as there are scores scattered around the city. They occupy vacant lots, are wedged between storefronts, and stand quietly behind bus stations, so ubiquitous that one soon begins to regard them as one does the many trees dotting the landscape.

Burmese temples with their half-dozen roofs and gingerbread eaves abound. Together with the distinctive Burmese-style chedis (also found in Lanna wats like those along Tha Phae Road) with their

foliage and golden rings like those of the 'long-necked' Karens (or Pa Dawn), they are found outside Lamphun and in Mae Hong Son.

Northern houses are generally built of teak with walls that slope outwards, not inwards like Central Plains homes. They are said to represent the water buffalo on which the people are so dependent: the columns representing the beast's stout legs, the outward sloping walls and roof – the massive body, and the crossed peaks called *galae* – the horns of the water buffalo.

Another feature is the *haem yon* placed over the doorway and

Chiang Mai, Lanna temple

representing testicles in which the guardian power of the house resides. When one moves house, he beats or destroys the *haem yon*.

In addition to the classical arts, Lanna artisans have refined decorative and practical crafts to a high degree. Lacquerware, silversmithing, ceramics, wood carving and umbrella-making are among the many arts found in the North, especially in Chiang Mai.

Hilltribe arts are simpler but more colourful and are primarily

created to adorn the body. Silver is crafted into belts, headdresses and other jewellery. Cloth is woven and embroidered with needlepoint or small patchwork in a wide variety of designs, most of which are derived

A Yao woman

from symbolic representations of nature. The style of embroidery – normally created by a young maiden as a test for prospective in-laws to determine her suitability as a wife – are distinctive among the different hilltribes and identify the tribes that have created them.

Religion

Theravada Buddhism is the North's dominant religion and its most prominent symbols are the wats and the monks in their saffron robes. Every young man becomes a monk for a short time to gain an understanding of his religion and to make merit so he will return as a more evolved being in the next life. Because women are not ordained as nuns, he also makes merit for his mother and sisters.

Each day at early light, silent monks walk barefoot through the villages and towns to receive rice and curries from Buddhists who wait in front of their homes. On Wan Phra (four times a month according to the lunar calendar), the faithful take food to the wat for the monks to eat after they have chanted ancient sermons in the Pali language. The three Buddhist holidays of Makha Puja, Visakha Puja, and Asalaha Puja are celebrated in all wats.

The North has many charming religious practices that recall the very human Hinduism of Bali. At certain times of the year, you will find tiny hillocks of sand in a temple courtyard, each with a small flag waving from its summit. This practice is a clever way of obtaining earth to raise the temple compound above the floodwaters. Each person who

Evening prayers at Doi Suthep

carries a handful of sand to the temple makes merit. It does not take too many handfuls before the temple has all the sand it needs for foundations or for the construction of new buildings.

The bodhi tree whose leaf ends in a distinctive, claw-like point, is the tree under which Buddha achieved Enlightenment. To prolong the lives of ancient trees, villagers bring poles to prop up its tired old limbs, giving the branches a comfortable support and earning merit for themselves in the process.

A spirit house

Taoist deities are worshipped by Chiang Mai's Chinese population. There is a small Thai and foreign Christian community and there are Islamic mosques throughout the town. Thai Buddhists cover all the bases, with a fervent belief in animism alongside their belief in Buddhism. Nearly every home has a small shrine where the spirits reside. Thais offer incense and flowers to these spirits to ensure protection in their daily lives.

The hilltribes are mostly animist, believing in spirits that protect the village and which must not be offended. The list of possible transgressions is lengthy. Some, like the Akha, build spirit gates which protect the village from malevolent ghosts. If one touches it or the column of a Karen house, one must donate a pig for sacrifice.

Northern Economy

Northern prosperity has traditionally been based upon rice. Other necessities came from small-scale trade over the mountains with China and other kingdoms. Early in this century, teak logging became a major industry. After the lapse of the foreign company leases the supply of trees began to dwindle and logging was banned in 1989, not that you can tell from the roar of chain saws that reverberate through the hills.

In the 1970s, King Bhumibol introduced a host of new crops to the North. Today, one passes fields of brussels sprouts, strawberries, cantaloupes, mushrooms and a dozen other crops never before grown. Coffee and tea plantations are plentiful, as are orchards of apples, peaches and other fruits normally associated with temperate climes.

Industry is being introduced primarily in the southern portion of Chiang Mai Valley and there is an air of boom-town about the larger towns with their new buildings and condominiums under construction. Unfortunately, much of the construction is dictated by economic considerations, with the result that the architectural integrity of Lanna has been seriously compromised.

Today, to see the North as a contiguous cultural unit, you must travel farther and farther from Chiang Mai.

Thai Values

While Buddhism is the prime influence shaping Thai moral behaviour there are several other important values. One is *sanuk*, a concept which translates roughly as 'fun'. Thais judge the value of an endeavour by the amount of *sanuk* it contains; anything not *sanuk* is to be avoided.

The Buddhist ideal of alleviating suffering has led to an attitude of *mai pen rai*: 'it doesn't matter' or 'no problem', accompanied by a shrug of the shoulders.

Wat and Village Visit Etiquette

Wats and Chinese shrines are open to all visitors. They do not charge admission fees but a small donation of even 10 baht to cover maintenance or restoration costs is appreciated.

Dress appropriately when visiting wats. Visitors in shorts and sleeveless shirts are forbidden entry. Take off your shoes before entering any wat building. Do not climb on the chedis or treat the Buddha images disrespectfully. You may photograph monks, wats,

Thai Yai man

22

Chedi at Wat Saen Fang

images, and all Buddhist ceremonies. When in doubt, though, ask for permission first.

If invited into a Thai home, remove your shoes at the door, *wai* the host and avoid stepping on the door sill where spirits are believed to reside. The *wai* is the traditional Thai greeting in which both hands are placed together, palm to palm, close to the body. The head is slightly bowed and the Thai word for greetings and farewell, *Sawasdee*, is said while performing the *wai*. Most Thais *wai* each other when they meet, although some modern ones may have adopted the western handshake.

Women should not touch monks or even brush against them. Thai monks take vows of chastity which prohibit their being touched by women, including their mothers. It is also insulting to touch another person on the head, point one's feet at him or step over him.

Hilltribe Culture and Etiquette

Hilltribes are animists and maintain a separate room in their houses for bones and other spirit objects. Some very good rules are offered by John R. Davies in his book *A Trekker's Guide to the Hilltribes of Northern Thailand*:

Take photographs only after asking permission.

Do not touch the altar or attempt to sleep under or near it.

A star-shaped bamboo sign, normally placed above the main door, means that permission should be asked before entering.

Mr. Davies suggests observing these tribal rules:

Buddhism

Prince Siddartha was born in Lumbini, southern Nepal, in 543 B.C. He lived a life of luxury, marrying a princess and fathering a child. It was only as an adult that he ventured beyond the palace walls where he saw a poor man, a sick man, and a dead man. Disturbed by this suffering, he left his luxurious life to become an ascetic.

Deciding that fasting was not the path to salvation, he began meditating. While meditating to reach Enlightenment, he was tempted by demons, a scene called *The Battle with Mara* that is normally depicted on the interior back walls of *wats*. He preached a doctrine of moderation (called the Middle Way), urging people to avoid extremes and remain indifferent to desire as a means of eliminating personal suffering. His life and final incarnations before being born as the Buddha are normally depicted on the side interior walls of a *viharn*.

23

A hilltribe house

Karens normally receive foreigners only on the verandah. It is taboo to touch stumps or burnt trees in the swidden areas.

Enter a Hmong home only if invited by a male inhabitant; if there are none, then the woman of the house can admit you.

Avoid touching or leaning against the stove in a Yao house for fear of offending spirits that reside in it. Do not touch the sacred posts around a Lahu temple as they are a source of blessing.

Never touch the house posts or the entrance gates to Akha villages. Accept any offer to enter a house and take any refreshment offered to you. Men should not enter the women's sections of the houses.

Outsiders may not enter the bedrooms, touch the altar or sleep with their heads towards the fire in a Lisu house. Foreign men and women cannot sleep together as they are usually placed in the guest room which also holds the altar; the male should sleep in the main room. Never stand in the doorway with your feet either side of it.

A Lahu girl on her family verandah

Historical Highlights

3,500 BC: Bronze Age culture created by an unknown people flourishes at Ban Chieng in Thailand's northeast.

8th-13th century: Migrants from China arrive in north Thailand administered by the Khmer empire from Cambodia.

1238: Khmer power wanes and Thais establish an independent nation based at Sukhothai.

1262, 1296: King Mengrai founds Chiang Rai and Chiang Mai.

1350: Farther south on the Chao Phya River, a new power emerges at Ayutthaya that supplants Sukhothai's dominance.

1451 and 1508: Chiang Mai wars with Ayutthaya.

1545: A gigantic earthquake destroys parts of Chiang Mai including the upper portion of the great chedi of Wat Chedi Luang.

1558: Chiang Mai defeated and occupied intermittently for two centuries by Burma.

1598: Ayutthaya defeats and occupies Chiang Mai but subsequently loses it to Burma.

1767: After repeated attempts, Burmese armies raze Ayutthaya. The Thai army regroups at Thonburi and for 15 years wars with the Burmese, Laotians and Vietnamese.

1774: Chiang Mai abandoned.

1782: The wars subside. General Chakri assumes the throne. Taking the name of Rama I, he moves his capital across the river to Bangkok.

1796: Prince Kawila re-populates Chiang Mai.

1809: Bangkok's major buildings are completed, Rama II re-creates the literature and arts that were destroyed at Ayutthaya.

1851: King Mongkut, the monarch of *The King and I*, ascends the throne after 27 years as a Buddhist monk. He sets Thailand on the path towards modernisation.

1868-1910: King Chulalong korn continues his father's initiatives and Siam moves into the 20th century. By political manoeuvering, he preserves national sovereignty, making Thailand the only Southeast Asian nation to escape colonisation.

1874: Bangkok begins to administer Chiang Mai through a royal commissioner.

1910-1925: King Vajiravudh concentrates on political reforms, giving greater freedom to his people, and encouraging criticism of government policies.

1921: The railway from Bangkok to Chiang Mai is completed.

1932: A revolution in Bangkok replaces absolute monarchy with a constitutional monarchy.

1939: Chiang Mai is upgraded to a province and ruled directly from Bangkok.

1941-45: Second World War: Thailand is occupied by the Japanese.

1950 - 1972: On May 5, Ananda's young brother, Prince Bhumibol is crowned King. There follows a succession of coup d'etat and military-backed governments. In the 1960s, Thailand experiences an economic boom as a result of investment by the U.S. in support of the Indochina war.

1973: A massive rising of students in Bangkok against the rule of the Three Tyrants ends in bloodshed. King Bhumibol appoints a neutral government.

1991: A group of three senior military officers seize power. Large demonstrations in Bangkok in favour of democracy are dispersed by military force. Many die or disappear. King Bhumibol selects Anand Panyarachun to form an interim government prior to elections.

1992: Elections are held, Chuan Leekpai becomes Prime Minister.

Day 12

Although Thai Airways International offers six or more daily flights to Chiang Mai it is more fun to travel by train. The day train requires 13 hours and lots of stamina but in the winter and the monsoon seasons, the arduous ride is compensated for by wonderful views of green trees and rice fields. In the hot season (late February through May), the fields are parched and unattractive.

The day train departs Bangkok's Hualampong Station at 6.35am and arrives in Chiang Mai at 8.05pm Conversely it leaves Chiang Mai at 6.35am and arrives in Bangkok at 8.05pm. Three very comfortable overnight sleeper trains run daily between Bangkok and Chiang Mai, leaving at 3pm, 6pm and at 7.40pm – this being the Nakhon Ping Express. They arrive at 5.15am, 7am and 8am respectively. There is also the sit-up only Sprinter leaving at 8.10am, arriving 5pm. Although you board after dark, you have more hours of light the next morning to enjoy the climb to the 1,352-m (1,480-yds) tunnel through the Khun Tan Hills. The station just beyong the tunnel is the highest point on the Royal Thai Railway system, 578m (1,900ft). Wild orchids and roast chicken for sale here.

Return trains leave Chiang Mai at 4.40pm, 8.40pm and 9.05pm (the Nakhon Ping Express) arriving Bangkok at 6am, 10.25am and 9.40am respectively. The Sprinter departs at 7.50pm and should get in to Bangkok at 6.25am next morning. Choose from first and second class air-conditioned cars or second class fan-cooled cars. Reserve all seats at Bangkok's Hualampong Station at Rama IV Road.

In the itineraries that follow, 'H' means Highway number and 'KM' refers to the kilometre post number by the side of the road.

Bangkok, Hualampong Station

Day ①

Chiang Mai City Tour

A day to savour the flavour and layout of Chiang Mai and its handicrafts. Spend the day exploring the area between the city wall and the river.

Ease into the morning. If you haven't just stepped off a plane or had breakfast at your hotel, make **Croissant** your first stop. Located at 318 Tha Phae Road, it opens at 7.30am and, as its name suggests, serves great croissants and coffee plus a selection of snacks. Keep it light as you will have an early lunch.

After breakfast, exit left and walk next door to the first of four wats you will visit within the city walls. These are not the most stunning of Chiang Mai's temples but they give a good introduction to the dominant architectural styles of the North. **Wat Chetawan**, with its three Burmese-style chedis, is undergoing extensive reconstruction. It may be several years before the main hall (viharn) is ready for its superb woodcarved gable to be restored to where it belongs.

Cross the street to **Wat Mahawan**. Perched on its wall are Burmese-style figures which guard a Burmese-style chedi and *viharn* (sermon hall). Compare the *viharn* with the *bot* (ordination hall marked by the six boundary stones around it) which is in the Lanna or northern style.

On the same side of the street, about 150m (165yds) to the east (against the traffic) is **Wat Boopharam**. Its new viharn is an odd mixture of styles, not at all harmonious. Under the Lanna-style roof is a square tower atop a blocky structure that is all filigree and frippery. The building holds

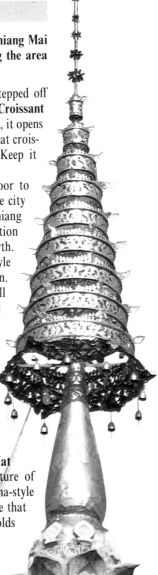

Wat Chetawan spire

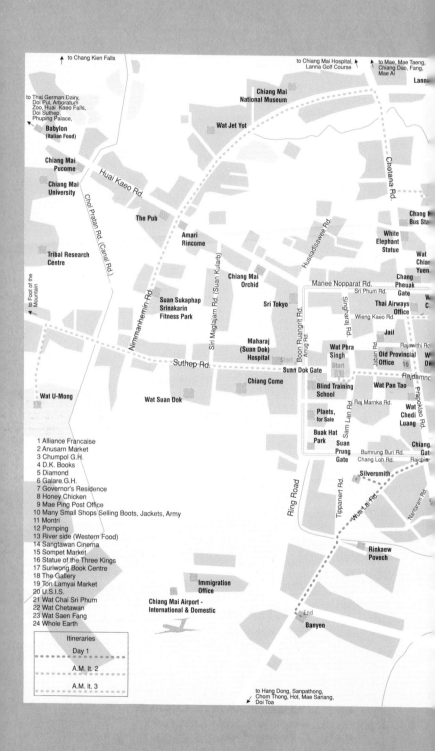

to Chang Kien Falls

to Chiang Mai Hospital,
Lanna Golf Course

to Mae, Mae Taeng,
Chiang Dao, Fang,
Mae Ai

Lanna

Chiang Mai
National Museum

to Thai German Dairy,
Doi Pui, Arboratum
Zoo, Huai Kaeo Falls,
Doi Suthep,
Phuping Palace,

Wat Jet Yot

Babylon
(Italian Food)

Chotana Rd.

Chiang Mai
Pucome

Huai Kaeo Rd.

Chiang Mai
University

Chang
Bus Sta

Chol Pratan Rd. (Canal Rd.)

The Pub

White
Elephant
Statue

Wat
Chiar
Yuen

Amari
Rincome

Hussadisawee Rd.

Tribal Research
Centre

Chang
Pheuak
Gate

Manee Nopparat Rd.

Chiang Mai
Orchid

Sri Phum Rd.

W
C.

to Foot of the
Mountain

Nimmanhemin Rd.

Siri Magiajam Rd. (Suan Kularb)

Thai Airways
Office

Singharaj Rd.

Suan Sukaphap
Srinakarin
Fitness Park

Sri Tokyo

Boon Ruangrit Rd.

Wieng Kaeo Rd.

Jail

Arug Rd.

Rawithi Ro

Jaban Rd.

Maharaj
(Suan Dok)
Hospital

Wat Phra
Singh

Old Provincial
Office

W
Di

Suthep Rd.

Start

16

Suan Dok Gate

Start

Rajdamno

Chiang Come

Blind Training
School

Wat Pan Tao

Prapokiao Rd.

Wat U-Mong

Wat Suan Dok

Raj Marnka Rd.

Wat
Chedi
Luang

Sam Lan Rd.

Plants,
for Sale

Buak Hat
Park

Chiang
Gat

1 Alliance Francaise
2 Anusarn Market
3 Chumpol G.H.
4 D.K. Books
5 Diamond
6 Galare G.H.
7 Governor's Residence
8 Honey Chicken
9 Mae Ping Post Office
10 Many Small Shops Selling Boots, Jackets, Army
11 Montri
12 Pornping
13 River side (Western Food)
14 Sangtawan Cinema
15 Sompet Market
16 Statue of the Three Kings
17 Suriwong Book Centre
18 The Gallery
19 Ton Lamyai Market
20 U.S.I.S.
21 Wat Chai Sri Phum
22 Wat Chetawan
23 Wat Saen Fang
24 Whole Earth

Suan
Prung
Gate

Bumrung Buri Rd.

Chang Loh Rd.

Rajchian

Silversmith

Ring Road

Tippanert Rd.

Huai Lai Rd.

Nantaram Rd.

Rinkaew
Povech

Immigration
Office

Chiang Mai Airport -
International & Domestic

End

Banyen

Itineraries

Day 1

A.M. It. 2

A.M. It. 3

to Hang Dong, Sanpathong,
Chom Thong, Hot, Mae Sariang,
Doi Toa

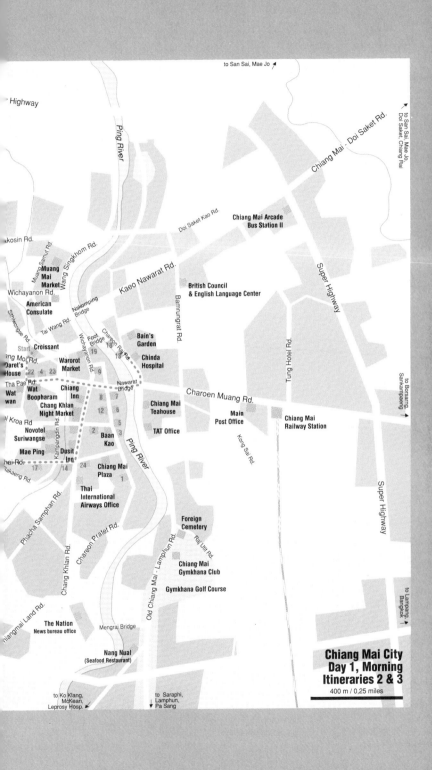

to San Sai, Mae Jo

Highway

Ping River

to San Sai, Mae Jo
to San Sai, Doi Saket,
Doi Saket Rd.

Chiang Mai - Doi Saket Rd.

Doi Saket Kao Rd.

Chiang Mai Arcade
Bus Station II

akosin Rd.

Muang Samut Rd.

Wang Singkhorn Rd.

Muang
Mai
Market

Kaeo Nawarat Rd.

British Council
& English Language Center

Wichayanon Rd.

American
Consulate

Nakornping
Bridge

Super Highway

Tai Wang Rd.

Foot
Bridge

Charoen Rat Rd.

Bain's
Garden

Bamrungrat Rd.

ang Moi Rd.

Start

Croissant

19

18

Wichayanon Rd.

Chinda
Hospital

Tung Hotel Rd.

Daret's
House

22   4   23

Warorot
Market

13

9

Nawarat
Bridge

to Borsang,
Sankampaeng

Tha Pae Rd.

Wat
Boopharam

Chiang
Inn

8   7

Charoen Muang Rd.

Wat
wan

11

6

Chiang Mai
Teahouse

Main
Post Office

Chiang Mai
Railway Station

Chang Khlan
Night Market

12

5

i Kroa Rd.

Novotel
Suriwangse

2

Baan
Kao

3

TAT Office

Kong Sai Rd.

Kampangdin Rd.

Mae Ping

Dusit
Inn

ai Rd.

17

14

Super Highway

akaeng Rd.

24

Chiang Mai
Plaza

1

Ping River

Thai
International
Airways Office

Phacha Samphan Rd.

Chang Khlan Rd.

Charoen Prater Rd.

Old Chiang Mai - Lamphun Rd.

Rai Uti Rd.

Foreign
Cemetery

Chiang Mai
Gymkhana Club

Gymkhana Golf Course

to Lampang,
Bangkok

Chiangmai Land Rd.

The Nation
News bureau office

Mengrai Bridge

Nang Nual
(Seafood Restaurant)

to Ko Klang,
McKean,
Leprosy Hosp.

to Saraphi,
Lamphun,
Pa Sang

Chiang Mai City
Day 1, Morning
Itineraries 2 & 3

400 m / 0,25 miles

what the abbot claims is the world's largest teak Buddha. The temple's prize building is the small wooden viharn to the right. Stucco decorations have been skillfully laid atop wood and topped with a Lanna roof. The interior holds a large and a small gilded Buddha image. Once inside, you are transported to another world bearing no reference to the traffic rushing by outside.

Cross the road and browse at D K Book House for magazines, maps, books on Thai history, language, etc before continuing on to **Wat Saen Fang** whose entrance gate looks like a separate temple in itself. Follow the undulating *naga* balustrade to the inner courtyard that holds a tall Burmese-style chedi defended by stucco *singhas* (mythical lions) that share guard duties with several antique cannons. Beneath the windows of the Lanna-Burmese viharn are handsome panels depicting mythical beasts. Decorating the eastern gables are fine carvings. To the west, along the roofline of the new *ubolsot* are some lovely praying disciples.

Back on Tha Phae Road turn left and after about 300m (330yds) turn right on to Chang Khlan Road (Creeping Elephant Road). This road not only accommodates the celebrated so-called **Night Bazaar** (to which you will return on an evening trip later) but also a host of restaurants and three large hotels. Choose one for a light lunch and to give your legs a rest.

After lunch, continue your walk along Chang Khlan Road until you reach the traffic lights at a crossroad. Cross over to the Caltex petrol station and hail a *tuk-tuk* (three-wheeled motorised trishaw). Ask to be taken to **Banyen Silver Shop** at 86/1-3 Wua Lai Road.

Chiang Mai was once a collection of villages, many of them devoted to a particular craft. **Wua Lai** was the silversmiths' village. Although most of the shops have moved to the San Kamphaeng Road area, the back streets still resound with the tap-tapping of hammers in home workshops. Banyen Silver Shop has a rather small collection of modern and antique jewellery but it is the starting point for a wander through the side *soi*.

Walk down the lane next to it marked Wua Lai Soi 2. Along it you will find a number of silverworking studios. At No. 28, you can watch the artisans at work under the house and then buy superbly crafted silver bowls in the living room at prices lower than those in shops. Alternatively, walk to Wua Lai Soi 3 to the **Siam Silverware Factory** (signs point the way to House No. 5) which offers a wide selection of items.

Catch a samlor down Wua Lai Road for about 1km (½ mile) to the **Lanna Folk Museum** on the left. In a lovely garden, the 130-year-old Lanna-style **Galae House** (Daily 10am–4pm, except Thursday), that formerly sat on the banks

eft, Main viharn of Wat Boopharam

Lanna folk museum

of the Ping River, serves as an ethnological museum, providing a glimpse of life in a former age. You can climb up the steps of Galae House and take a look at the antique household utensils, farm equipment and lovely lacquerware items on display.

In 1990, a fire destroyed the **Banyen Museum** on Wua Lai Road. Fortunately, Mrs Banyen had already begun moving items to her shop. But the old bicycle which she used in the 1950s to peddle her wares to those staying at the old Railway Hotel (built in 1919) was destroyed in the blaze. Her shop (Tel: 274-007, Daily 8.30am–4.30pm) is located opposite Tantraphan Airport Plaza which is near the traffic lights at the intersection of the road to Chom Thong and the City Circular Road.

Banyen's primary appeal is that it makes shopping fun. Statues

Mrs Banyen

lie under trees and lean against old wooden houses, cluttering every corner so that when you least expect it, you stumble across a treasure. If nothing more, it is a pleasure to wander through the compound. Workers work, sleepy cats curl up on convenient statues and there is a wonderful air of informality about the entire yard. These are not antiques but very credible copies sold as home decor items. Prices are quite reasonable.

After freshening up at your hotel, have dinner overlooking the Ping River at **Riverside Restaurant** on Charoen Rat

Banyen woodcarving factory

Road. You may want to return here on another night to enjoy the live music and the lively crowd which the restaurant and bar attract every night.

Exit Riverside to the right, crossing the **Nawarat Bridge**. Walk one block and turn left into the heart of the famous **Chang Khlan Night Market**. Vendors crowd the sidewalks with a superb array of goods at very attractive prices. There are many stalls crowding the footpaths and a throng of vendors and visitors. A word of warning – keep a tight grip on your wallet or shoulder bag all the time.

Day 2

Handicraft Studios and Doi Suthep

A visit to handicraft studios and Chiang Mai's tallest hill with its stunning temple, the royal summer palace and a hilltribe village. A night-time ride through the city streets.

Breakfast at your hotel or on the banks of the Ping at River View Lodge at the end of Soi 2, Charoen Prathet Road. Then catch a bus or drive to **Borsang Village** heading for San Kamphaeng District. Red and white bus No. 2259 leaves from Chang Pheuak Bus Station, stopping in front of Bangkok Bank on Charoen Muang Road. It might be easiest to hire a *samlor* for the entire morning for about 200 baht.

The morning is devoted to watching how Chiang Mai's ancient crafts are created, and then shopping for bargains. The nine shops noted here lie along the road to Borsang and have studios that welcome visitors. A visit to all nine could easily turn a morning into a full day so you might want to pick and choose the crafts that interest you. Start just past the Superhighway intersection.

Napa Lacquerware, 8/2 San Kamphaeng Road (KM 5.2), Tel: 243-039. Chiang Mai residents will argue that the fame of Burmese lacquerware is undeserved; that the Burmese artisans were in fact Thais who were enslaved by the Burmese and forced to work in their studios. Nonetheless,

Lacquerware items

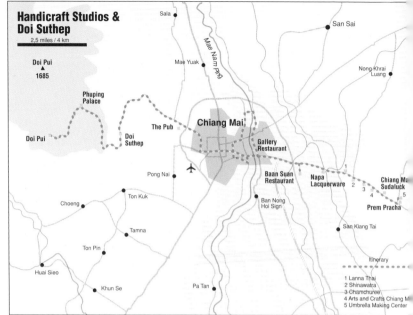

Sala
San Sai
Doi Pui
▲
1685
Mae Yuak
Nong Khrai
Luang
Phuping
Palace
The Pub
Chiang Mai
Doi Pui
Doi
Suthep
Gallery
Restaurant
Pong Nai
Baan Suan
Restaurant
Napa
Lacquerware
Chiang Mai
Sudaluck
Choeng
Ton Kuk
Ban Nong
Hoi Sign
Prem Pracha
Tamna
San Kiang Tai
Ton Pin
Itinerary
Huai Sieo
Khun Se
Pa Tan

1 Lanna Thai
2 Shinawatra
3 Chamchuree
4 Arts and Crafts Chiang M
5 Umbrella Making Center

Chiang Mai seems to have retained enough artisans of its own to produce some fine work. Lacquerware comes in two varieties: gold leaf on glossy black, and green and black designs on a dark red base. Once found only in royal households, the principal items – betel boxes, servings trays, jewellery boxes – are produced in intriguing shapes created from bamboo and overlaid with lacquer. The studio also produces trays and containers covered in dyed eggshell which has been crushed to create lovely mosaics.

Lanna Thai, 79 San Kamphaeng Road. (KM 6.1), Tel: 338-015/17. Silverware is another old Chiang Mai art. In addition to antique designs, the shop also produces hilltribe jewellery whose appeal lies less in its silver content (which is low) than in its artistry.

Shinawatra, 145/1-2 San Kamphaeng Road. (KM 7.1), Tel: 338-053/058. No craft is more representative of Thailand than Thai silk. Although generally associated with the Northeast, silk has found a home in the North's many workshops. Observe how the silkworms are raised on a diet of mulberry leaves, and how their cocoons are boiled and the filaments unwound and woven on hand looms into lengths of shimmering cloth.

Chamchuree Lapidary, 166/1 San Kamphaeng Road. (KM 7.5), Tel: 338-631. Burmese jade is imported in large quantities into northern Thailand where it is carved into pendants and other kinds of jewellery.

Gold brooch on violet silk

Arts & Crafts Chiang Mai, 172 San Kamphaeng Road. (KM 7.8), Tel: 331-977. Bronze-crafting is more prevalent in the Central Plains but the subjects are the same: Buddha images. Look at some of the fine images in Lanna temples where the art reached a zenith of perfection. Retail items range from religious to decorative.

Chiangmai Sudaluck, 99/9 San Kamphaeng Road. (KM 8.2), Tel: 338-006. With hills once covered in teak forests, it was natural that Chiang Mai would produce wood carvings. Skilled woodwork is apparent in every northern temple; wood carving is a tradition carried on in this shop's studios. The shop specialises in furniture and home decor items.

Umbrella Making Centre, 111/2 San Kamphaeng Road. (KM 9), Tel: 338-324. Borsang was once a tiny village where artisans laboured under their houses to craft bamboo, string and *sah* paper (made from the bark of the mulberry tree) into umbrellas that are a marvel of engineering. These were then painted with motifs from nature. The craft has since become an industry with a resultant loss of quality but the umbrellas are still produced by hand. A half-hour in an umbrella-making workshop is time well spent. This one, at the intersection with the road to Doi Saket, is the best known.

Prempracha's Collection, on San Kamphaeng Road. (KM 9), Tel: 338-540. Ceramics are another well-known northern

Applying sah paper onto the bamboo ribs of an umbrella

art, the most representative being celadon, a handsome light green glaze applied to lampstands, bowls and other items. Blue- and white-porcelain, earthenware and *bencharong* (five-colour pottery) are also produced here.

For lunch, return to KM 4 and turn left for Thai food in **Baan Suan** in a lovely garden 200m (230yds) away. Highly recommended.

The afternoon and early evening will be spent on **Doi Suthep**, the holy hill west of Chiang Mai. You may find it more convenient to rent a car for the afternoon as *tuk-tuks* are not allowed on the hill. If you prefer local transport, a mini-bus leaves from Tha Phae Road in front of the Bangkok Bank 100m (110yds) past the intersection with Chang Khlan Road) every 10 minutes for Doi Suthep, Phuping Palace and Doi Pui.

The steep road begins at the end of Huai Kaeo Road past the zoo. It winds for 12km (7½ miles) up the flanks of Doi Suthep (*Doi* means mountain) before reaching a parking lot. For the moment, forget the wat. Drive past the wat staircase and onto the road on the left which climbs through pine forests to **Phuping Palace**, 4km (2½ miles) farther on.

Phuping is a summer residence used by the Royal Family as a headquarters for overseeing development projects in northern Thai and hilltribe villages. When the Royal Family is not in residence, the beautiful flower gardens are open from 8.30am to 4pm to the public from Friday to Sunday and on official holidays. The gardens are well worth a visit.

Continue 3km (1¾ miles) to the Hmong village of **Doi Pui**. While it is very commercialised, enough of it remains to give you a flavour of hilltribe life to help you decide if you want to trek to one (see Excursions). As you walk through the streets, you will be accosted to buy items or give money. If you take a photograph of a Hmong in costume, you will be asked for money.

A hilltribe quilt

Especially interesting are the **Opium Museum** and the **Hilltribe Museum**. For centuries, the Hmong have been opium growers. The first museum documents how the crop is cultivated and processed, and displays some of the implements used in opium production.

In the Hilltribe Museum, the implements used in daily life are exhibited. It has historical significance in that many of the items have been replaced by more modern materials and are no longer used.

At about 4pm, return along the road to **Wat Phra That Doi Suthep** (superb views of it along the road), Chiang Mai's most

Right, gardens at Doi Pui

Naga stairway up Doi Suthep

famous temple. Perched high on the flank of the hill, 1,022m (3,000ft) above sea level, it has watched Chiang Mai's dramatic changes over the past 30 years. Aside from minor alterations, it has remained what it always was: a peaceful retreat that lends itself to contemplation (except for the days when it is overrun by tourists). No visit to Chiang Mai – even for those who have visited it a dozen times – is complete without a long drive up the hill to the base of its *naga* (serpent) staircase.

Although a funicular railway now glides to the top, resist the urge to take it. Instead, accumulate a bit of merit for yourself by climbing the 210 steps (304 from the parking lot) to the summit. You will enjoy the sense of relief when you reach the top.

According to legend, the temple's site was selected by an elephant. A monk named Sumana placed half of a Buddha relic on an elephant's back and set it loose. It was decided that when the elephant stopped walking, a temple would be built to house the gem. The elephant must have had a perverse streak because instead of stopping at an easy site, it began climbing the hill. One can imagine the mutters and muted curses of the people trying to keep up with it as they crashed through heavy jungle hot on its heels.

It seemed bent on walking to Burma but finally, to everyone's relief, it paused on the brow of the hill, trumpeted, turned around three times like a dog bedding down for the night, and lay down. This was where Wat Phra That Doi Suthep was built.

Take off your shoes and climb to the inner sanctuary. Women wearing shorts are barred from entering but they can rent sarongs for 10 baht near the entrance. Inside is a four-sided chedi with brass which, like Bangkok's Wat Arun, seems to symbolise the North.

Doi Suthep from afar

Keep an eye out for the small *hong*, or mythical swan, on the wire stretching from the pinnacle to the base of the chedi. Thai Buddhists bestow their own blessings on the chedi by filling with

Doi Suthep, main courtyard

water the cup which the swan holds in its beak.

They then turn the wheel on a pulley, raising the swan to the chedi's crown where a small projection tips the cup, spilling the water down the sides of this sacred monument.

The complex abounds in odd memorials to chickens and other beasts (whose models stroll unhindered around today). The viharns at either end hold some Buddha images, none of them of real merit;

the murals in the cloisters have been ruined by repeated restoration. At 5pm monks gather in the western viharn for the evening prayers.

Listen to the ethereal murmurings then exit the inner grounds. Ring the bells for good luck and walk to the balustrade to watch dusk gradually descend on Chiang Mai far below.

You have a choice for dinner: English or Thai-Chinese cuisine.

For English food, drive down the hill to **Huai Kaeo Road**. There, on the right, 150m

Chicken Statue at Doi Suthep

(164yds) before the intersection with the Superhighway, is **The Pub Restaurant** which serves typically English meals in a cozy dining room. In the winter, a fire blazes in the foyer for pre-prandial drinks.

For Thai-Chinese cuisine, go to the **Khrua Sabai** (Tel: 274-042) at the golf-driving range, opposite Airport Plaza. The food here is highly recommended.

After dinner, you may feel like walking round to the night bazaar on Chang Khlan to buy more presents even if you've wandered there before. Don't walk alone along unlit lanes and keep touts at bay. Ask at your hotel or guest house if there is anything for a visitor to see in the cultural line. There are ceremonies well worth observing at temples on certain full moon nights, or there is the Loy Krathong festival during the full moon in October or November. Or you could just sit at a table on the footpath with a thirst quencher and watch the world go by.

Morning Itineraries

1. Inner City Market Walk

You have to rise early for this one because the market is in full swing long before the sun comes up. Catch a tuk-tuk to Chiang Mai's oldest wet market, Ton Lamyai, at the end of Chang Moi Road next to the river. At one of the stalls, sip a morning glass of Thai coffee (Cafe Thai).

Then begin exploring. This is the traditional Thai supermarket where you can find anything you want. Fruits and vegetables, flowers, spices and freshly-butchered meats from the countryside pause here on their way to the kitchens and dining tables of the city. It is a great place to exercise your sense of smell and to gain a new and colourful dimension on Asian life.

Across the street to the west is the **Warorot Day Market**, a warren of alleys where all sorts of household items are sold. Wander in to see the things that Thais consider essential to their daily lives.

On another morning, you might want to explore the **Muang Mai market** just up the river past the Nakhon Ping Bridge. Bigger and more modern than Ton Lamyai, it is no less lively.

Ton Lamyai Market

Angels at the base of Wat Phra Singh library

2. Temples within the Old City Walls

A tour, by samlor or tuk-tuk of Wat Phra Singh, Wat Chedi Luang, Wat Pan Tao, Wat Duang Di, Wat Chiang Mun.

Flag down a *samlor* or, if you are impatient or pity the straining driver, a *tuk-tuk*. Bargain for a good price. If you feel really energetic, take a tuk-tuk to **Wat Phra Singh** and walk to the others, a total distance of about 2 km (1.2 miles).

Even from a distance, Wat Phra Singh, Chiang Mai's most famous temple after the Doi Suthep, is impressive. Sited at the T-intersection of Rajdamnoen and Singharaj Roads, its viharn just beyond the entrance gate, is stately.

Like many Lanna temples of northern Thailand, Wat Phra Singh has a balustrade that depicts a *naga* (serpent) with a *makara* emerging from its mouth. This is a motif commonly favoured by Khmer artists in temples of Thailand's northeast. The Buddha inside is rather ordinary but the

41

The gum tree whose fate is entwined with Chiang Mai's

ornate wood and mosaic pulpit on the left is worth a closer examination.

Exit the viharn, turn left to the beautiful library, a wooden Lanna-style building erected on an older base. Its stucco angels convey a tranquillity and delicacy matched only by those at Wat Jet Yot.

Directly behind the viharn is a beautiful wooden *bot* with a stunning stucco and gold entrance. Behind it is a chedi built by King Pha Yu in 1345 to hold the ashes of his father, King Kam Fu. In Sukhothai (and Sri Lankan) tradition, the structure rests on the backs of four brick and stucco elephants, one on each side.

The most beautiful building in the temple compound is the famous Phra Viharn Laikam to the left of the chedi. As with all *bot*s, its area of sanctuary is defined by six *bai sema*; these are unusual in being phallic-shaped. Of all of Chiang Mai's temple buildings, this is perhaps the most representative of Lanna-style architecture although it was built in 1811, rather late in the Lanna period. Intricately carved stucco door frames compete in beauty with the doors themselves, dominated by lacquer guardians.

Inside the Phra Viharn Laikam are murals painted in the last century which depict two stories. The one on the right wall is of *Saengthong*, an ancient Thai tale (not one of the *chadoks* as suggested elsewhere). Its most interesting subjects are the boys, buffaloes, and other delightful characters from life 200 years ago.

On the left wall is the story of the *Suphannahong*, a mythical swan which is an important figure seen frequently in northern art and architecture. Unfortunately, the mural is so badly damaged by water that it is indistinct. Small portions of it, though, give some idea of the grandeur of the original.

Exit Wat Phra Singh and head for **Wat Chedi Luang**, one of Chiang Mai's most impressive wats. Located on Phrapoklao Road, the fate of the tall gum tree just inside the entrance is linked to that of the city: According to legend, when the gum tree falls, so will Chiang Mai. It shades the city pillar which traditionally marks the geographic centre of a Thai town and from which the power that guards its inhabitants emanates.

The viharn is rather plain, holding a tall Standing Buddha flanked by two disciples. Of more interest are the framed pictures along the walls whose English-language captions explain the story of Buddha's life. These are worth reviewing in order to understand the Life of Buddha paintings found in other Chiang Mai temples.

The wat's most impressive structure is the huge chedi at the rear. Built in 1401 by King Saeng Muang Ma and raised to a height of 86m (282ft) by King Tilokaraja (the builder of Wat Jet Yot) in 1454, it was reduced to its present height of 42m (138ft) by a massive earthquake in 1545.

Unfortunately, the Fine Arts Department was allowed to work on a restoration and whilst not carrying out a complete reconstruction, it has managed to create one of the ugliest edifices for miles around, out of what was a ruined chedi of great beauty and which the people of Chiang Mai loved and greatly revered.

The viharn of **Wat Pan Tao**, next door to Chedi Luang, is a masterpiece of wood construction. Visible from the street, its fire-engine red doorway is crowned by a lovely Lanna peacock framed by golden serpents.

Wat Duang Di offers little but is a pleasant stop on the way to Wat Chiang Mun. Walk down Phrapoklao Road to a small *soi* (lane) on the right just before the corner of Rajawithi Road and the Provincial Law Court.

Wat Chedi Luang

Wat Chiang Mun on Rajapakinai Road is the oldest of the four principal temples within the city walls. Built in 1296, the year of the town's founding, its name translates as 'power of the city' suggesting its importance to Chiang Mai's early inhabitants. The courtyard is thought to have served as the home of King Mengrai while he was building his new capital. Its Lanna-style viharn, dating from the 19th century, is dec-

Left, the gables of the viharn at Wat Chedi Luang

Wat Chiang Mun

orated with an intricately-carved, three-headed elephant god, Erawan, as well as some superb carved teak panels on the gable. It holds several handsome bronze Buddha images from the Lanna and U-thong periods. If it is not open, it is worth asking one of the monks for the key to the temple.

The viharn on the right contains Chiang Mai's two most sacred Buddha images. The most important is the Phra Setang Khamani, the small crystal figure on the left, said to command the clouds. In drought years, Chiang Mai residents propitiate it to bring rain. On the festive day of Songkran, it is carried around the city in a grand procession and water is poured over it to bring rain in the coming rice-planting season. It is also thought to protect the city from fire. It was taken from a temple in Haripunchai (now known as Lamphun) in 1281 by King Mengrai.

A second image, the finely-carved Phra Sila, on the right side of the altar, is thought to have been brought from India around the end of the first millenium. On the viharn walls are murals depicting the Life of Buddha in the upper panels and the *chadoks* (previous incarnations of Buddha) in the lower panels.

Of particular interest is the 15th-century square chedi at the rear of the compound. Reflecting Sri Lankan and Sukhothai tradition, the chedi appears to be supported on the backs of 15 elephant caryatids built into the base of the structure, as is found in several Sukhothai and Kampaengphet chedis.

Wat Chiang Mun, chedi

Look also at the modern *ho trai* or library containing Buddhist scriptures. It sits to the left of the chedi and is a masterpiece of wood carving and lacquer decoration. In the Central Plains, a structure like this would sit atop columns in a pond so the sacred manuscripts would not be eaten by termites. It holds a small museum with lacquer manuscript cabinets, Buddha images, pipes, and old Thai money.

In the far left-hand corner of the compound, the plain, wide wooden doors of the bot conceal some superb Lanna and U-thong period bronze Buddha images.

3. Temples Beyond Chiang Mai

A visit to some of the quieter, statelier temples on the outskirts of the city, touring Wat Suan Dok, Wat U-Mong, Wat Jet Yot, Wat Ku Tao.

Part of the appeal of the wats outside the city is their air of tranquillity suggesting an earlier, quieter age. Within their walls, you can experience the Buddhist calm with which the temples were originally invested.

The first of these lies on the left along Suthep Road; bus No. 1 heading west out of Suan Dok Gate will take you there. Get off at

Wat Ku Tao

Monks Approach To Chat

While wandering around temples, you will often be approached by young monks asking questions. Their interest is in practising English but they are often a wealth of information about village life (many are country boys) and daily temple routines. Unless they are clutching books soliciting donations, take a few moments to talk with them. Such encounters can often lead to long-term friendships.

the temple gate 300m (330yds) beyond the traffic lights.

Founded in 1383, **Wat Suan Dok** (the Flower Garden Temple) is originally thought to have been a royal pleasure garden. Legend says that the Sri Lankan monk Sumana was directed in a dream to dig beneath an old chedi in Sukhothai. His shovel unearthed a series of boxes within boxes, the innermost containing a glowing gem. When the Sukhothai king attempted to use the gem's miraculous powers for his own gain, it stopped glowing. Sumana then took it to Chiang Mai where King Ku Na erected a chedi in his flower garden to hold it. As it was being buried, the gem split in two, much to everyone's consternation. One half was buried in the chedi and the other half was transported on elephant back to Doi Suthep where a second chedi was built.

Recent restoration of the viharn has resulted in a cold shell of concrete and iron grills. Even this, however, fails to detract from the beauty of its 500-year-old Buddha image and others behind it. It is in the courtyard to the west, however, that its true appeal lies. Here, next to an elegant chedi built in 1372 and restored in 1931,

is a garden of brilliant white chedis containing the ashes of Chiang Mai nobles. It is an impressive sight at any hour of the day but especially at sunset.

Continue along Suthep Road through the Ton Payom market area, cross the canal and after 500m (550yds) turn left for Wat U-mong, 1km (½ mile) away.

In the days when the valley floor was covered in forests and travel was difficult, **Wat U-mong** was a quiet meditation retreat, a quality it has maintained to this day. Recently restored, it sits among beau-

tiful plane and teak trees that evoke the peace of the past. Sit for a while and listen to the leaves rustling and the cicadas singing. There is an open zoo next door.

Return to Suthep Road, turn right and at the second lot of traffic lights, turn left into Nimmanahaemin da Road. Cross

Wat U-mong

over the intersection at the Amari Rincome Hotel corner on to the Superhighway, and after 1km (½ mile), turn left again to enter **Wat Jet Yod**.

Founded by King Tilokaraja in 1455, this unusual structure (whose name translates as 'seven spires') is a replica of the Mahabodi Temple in Bodhgaya, India, where Buddha gained enlightenment.

Soon after the completion of the temple, King Tilokaraja arranged for the 8th World Buddhist Council to meet in Chiang Mai in 1477. The meeting was attended by more than 100 monks from various countries. In 1566, however, Wat Jet Yod was badly damaged when the Burmese conquered Chiang Mai and pillaged it.

Continue along the Superhighway to Chang Pheuak Road, turn

right and then left on Soi 6, opposite Thai Thanu Bank. **Wat Ku Tao** is at the end of the lane behind a wall guarded by celestial lions. The wat's viharn is plain but its unusual chedi commands atten-tion. Viewers disagree on whether it resembles five pumpkins or five monks' alms bowls in descending size, stacked atop each other. The source of inspiration for the design is unknown and unparal-leled. Look closely at the decoration: flowers fashioned from ceramic shards. Again, one of the temple's attractions is its tranquility. Sit under the banyan tree and contemplate its peace.

From here, return to your hotel.

Wat Suan Dok, viharn

Café Thai and Patongkoh

4. Dawn on Doi Suthep

Watch sunrise over Chiang Mai from Doi Suthep with its chanting nuns and singing jungle birds. Leave at about 5am for sunrise at 6.30am.

Doi Suthep is at its best at dawn. At this hour, there are few taxis so you will need a motorcycle or car. Dawn is too early for the vendors and most tourists so you have the place virtually to yourself. Nuns chant *sutras* in the northern viharn and jungle birds sing, creating a mystical atmosphere that is everything the exotic Orient is meant to be.

Walk to the parapet to watch the sky lighten and the sun rise over Chiang Mai. Sunrise is usually at 6.30am by which time the temple will be stirring to life. From the temple, drive carefully down the hill and have breakfast at your hotel or near Tha Phae Gate, where you will find JJ Restaurant in the Montri Hotel, or, on the other side of the moat, the popular and long-established Daret's House.

If you are really adventurous, head into the **Ton Lamyai market** and have a breakfast of Thai coffee and *patongkoh*, a Chinese pastry. The market is on the riverbank at the end of Chang Moi Road. If you are not sufficiently awake, order *Khai Luek*, a barely-boiled egg in a drinking glass over which you splash a bit of soy sauce. Some Thais lace it with Mekong whisky. That ought to wake you up.

Blushing from the rising sun

Right, Doi Suthep, warrior statue

48

Afternoon Itineraries

5. Nature Walk

A stroll through Chiang Mai Zoo and Botanical Gardens to see exotic tropical animals and trees. By local bus.

The **Chiang Mai Zoo** (Daily 8am–5pm. Tel: 222-479) began as a menagerie of family pets in the home of Harold Young, whose parents were well-known missionaries from northern Burma. It soon outgrew the house and was donated to the city which created a park at the foot of Doi Suthep on Huai Kaeo Road.

The zoo houses a wide variety of Asian and African animals and includes a 84-rai (34-acre) open zoo where you can wander among the more harmless creatures. There are also camping facilities.

Next door is the **Huai Kaeo Arboretum**, (Daily 8.30am–4.30pm, Free admission) a rainforest where the trees and plants are labelled. This is an excellent place to learn the names of tropical plants you will encounter on a trek in the hills.

6. Ancient Arts

Spend the afternoon learning the arts and customs of the two cultures that dominate the north: the hilltribes and the Lanna. Take a tuk-tuk to the Chiang Mai University.

To reach the **Tribal Research Centre** at Chiang Mai University, enter the Huai Kaeo Road gate and check the mapboard on the left for directions. The centre displays costumes, utensils and weapons of major hilltribe groups as well as maps showing the locale of each.

Meo mother and child

View from the Ping River

The **Chiang Mai Museum** (Open 9am–4pm. Closed Monday, Tuesday and on official holidays) on the Superhighway near Wat Jet Yot provides a superb overview of Lanna art. Among its prize exhibits is a huge Chiang Saen-style bronze Buddha head 3m (10ft) tall and a beautiful footprint inlaid with intricate mother-of-pearl. The museum also offers a catholic representation of northern artifacts ranging from hilltribe costumes to items used in the everyday life of a Lanna hilltribe.

7. Massage Lessons

Take a 5 to 10 day course on traditional Thai massage.

Traditional Thai massage is an invigorating way of relieving that knot in your back or anywhere else on your body. The ancient art form works on the same principle as acupressure and your body is pummeled and punched at strategic points to balance the body's energies. For lessons on traditional Thai massage, take a *tuk-tuk* to the **Institute of Thai Massage** (Monday–Friday 9am–4pm) at 17/7 Morakot Road, Santitham. Tel: 218-632.

8. Up the Ping River

An afternoon cruise up the Ping River. Tuk-tuk to boat landing.

Up the Ping on a lazy afternoon. The **River View Lodge** at 25 Chareon Prathet, Soi 4 (on the river) offers a leisurely two-hour boat ride 5km (3 miles) up the Ping River.
 View old Thai-style houses and the city skyline. Maximum four persons. The boat leaves the Lodge pier at any time from 9am–4pm by prior arrangement. Phone 271-109 or 271-110.

EXCURSIONS

9. Elephants and Bamboo Rafts

Watch elephants at work at Chiang Dao Camp then raft down the Ping River. If you have your own transportation, continue to Chiang Dao caves. Get around by local bus or car.

A bus leaves the Chang Pheuak Gate Bus Station at 7am, crossing a flat valley and climbing the northern valley wall. Farm houses and neat squares of rice or vegetable fields fall away on either side of the road. Soon, the bus is twisting and turning along the bends high above the beautiful Ping River.

Tell the driver you want to get off at KM 56 (watch the kilometre posts along the road just in case). You will arrive at the **Chiang Dao Elephant Camp** in ample time for the 9am show; if you get the 7.30am bus you will still be in time for the 10am show.

The programme begins with a majestic procession of elephants up the Ping River. Then it is bath time with much splashing and trumpeting. Later, the elephants demonstrate how they move large teak logs as if they were matchsticks, a skill they have employed for more than a century in the teak forests of the North.

After the 40-minute show, guests are invited to take a short elephant-back amble around the grounds. Perched high in a wooden howdah you gain a unique view of the scenery and an impressive close-up view of the huge beast's musculature and thick hide. Strongly recommended.

After the show, have a snack at the open air restaurant overlooking the Ping River and then negotiate with boatmen for a 4km (2½ miles) ride on a bamboo raft down the Ping to **Tha Rua**. The narrow raft holds four persons squatting on low benches as a boatman poles the craft on a leisurely 45-minute journey through tropical vegetation and, appropriately, elephant grass.

At the journey's end, walk the short distance to the Chiang Mai-Fang Highway and hail a bus for the ride to Chiang Mai.

Washing elephants

52

Chiang Dao Caves, entrance

If you have parked at the Elephant Camp, catch a bahtbus to retrieve it and then head up the highway to Chiang Dao. About 500m (550yds) beyond the town, turn left 5km (3 miles) through villages and tobacco fields to **Chiang Dao Caves**.

The caves are a series of rooms reached by climbing stairs and, in one instance, a ladder through a narrow passage. Pay the small entrance fee and get a guide to accompany you. Enter the large gallery. The caves extend for more than 10km, but do not attempt to explore beyond the Reclining Buddha which is a 10-minute walk away, following the electric light wires.

Return to your vehicle, stop for a welcome drink under the tamarind trees and then return to Chiang Mai. There are several shops along the way selling farm implements, fishing baskets, and other village utensils. These make unusual, lightweight gifts.

Mae Sa Valley Resort, flower garden

10. Samoeng and Mae Sa valleys

This varied day takes you through a beautiful valley to visit an elephant camp, flower gardens, butterflies, orchids, and an old museum. You will need a car or motorcycle to get around.

Travel south on H 108 for 16km (10 miles) towards Hang Dong, then turn right onto H 1269, travelling for 2km (1¼ miles) to **Wat Ton Kwen** on the left (a roadside sign indicates the turning). This peaceful little temple amid palm trees is a lovely example of Lanna architecture. Its wooden *bot*, guarded by a pair of handsome stucco *nagas*, is surrounded on three sides by an open cloister, an unusual architectural treatment. The decoration on the bot and the viharn in front of it is especially fine.

H 1269 loops around behind Doi Suthep. At KM 38 (there is a police booth on the left) continue straight down the hill into **Samoeng**, a pretty valley town with some lovely, tree-shaded back streets. Have an iced coffee in a roadside restaurant and return to KM 38, turning turn left onto H 1096 at the police booth.

After 14km (8¼ miles), pass through Pong Yang Village and at KM 13 enter the top of the Mae Sa Valley Resort. Take a break to stretch your legs, admire the flowers and have some refreshments. At KM 10 you will reach the site of the Elephant Camp, with shows at 8am and 9.40am. With an early start you might catch the 9.40am show. If you are a late starter, I suggest you tackle this itinerary anticlockwise and visit Mae Sa Valley first, taking in the 8am elephant show before continuing to complete the Samoeng Loop in a more leisurely manner.

At KM 7 look out for **Mae Ram Orchid Nursery and Butterfly Farm**. Dozens of varieties of orchids are nurtured under netting. One can buy seedlings with full instructions for their care — but check plant quarantine regulations if taking to another country.

The **Chiang Mai Snake Farm** is at KM 5, and a bit further on you will see a board pointing to the Mae Sa Bronze Foundry, just before Lanna House Antiques and Handicrafts. Opposite the Shell petrol station there is a large

Map: Samoeng and Mae Sa valleys — 8 km / 5 miles

Labels: Thung Pa Haeo • Oi • Mae Rim • Mae Tao Hai • Tin Do • Butterfly Farm • Mae Sa House Collection • Kong Khak Luang • Pong Yang Elephant Camp • Tai • Mai Nai • Mae Cho • Nan Rin • Nam Mae Sa • Mae Rim Orchid Nursery • Wang Pong • Mae Sa Valley Resort • Sala • Samoeng • Doi Pui ▲ 1685 • Phuping Palace • Chang Klan • Pang Yang • Nam Mae • Doi Pui • Chiang Mai • Nam Mae Khanin • Thung Pong • Mae Hae Nai • Doi Mon Pha Sing ▲ 1005 • Tha Chang • Huai Sieo • Ton Kuk • Sop Hual Yao • Wat Ton Kwen • Pa Tan • Ping River • Nam Phrao • Nong Ha • Pa Chi • Hang Dong • Saraphi

space for parking cars in front of the **Mae Sa Butterfly and Orchid Farm**, with **Mae Sa Kitchen** attached, well worth a visit.

The Butterfly Farm raises a large variety of beautiful butterflies in a spacious garden around which you can wander. The farm has a shop which sells framed specimens; although after seeing them flying so freely you may not have the heart to buy them stretched out on cotton.

Were it not for the setting, the **Mae Sa Collection House** could be somewhere in Europe since some of the exhibits are family heirlooms collected on trips abroad. Nonetheless, the Thai-style houses contain amusing items like a clock that runs backwards, and an early model of a motorcycle.

Wat Ton Kwen

To return to Chiang Mai, drive along H 1096 another 3km (1¾ miles) to H 108, turn right and within 16km (5 miles) you will enter Chiang Mai by Chang Pheuak Gate.

Lamphun

Moat — to Chiang Mai

Kwang River

to Wat Chamathew

Museum

Wat Phra That Haripunchai

Footbridge

Wat Prayoon

to Lampang

Kwang River

Moat

A ride through a corridor of beautiful gum trees and a visit to the quiet old capital of the 7th- century Haripunchai empire. By local bus.

Lamphun, the beautiful old capital of the Haripunchai empire, lies 26km (16 miles) south of Chiang Mai. To get there, you can take a bus from the stop on the Chiang Mai-Lamphun Road, about 200m (220yds) south of Nawarat Bridge.

This is one of the prettiest drives in the kingdom: Just south of Chiang Mai, the Chiang Mai-Lamphun Road runs between twin rows of magnificent tall gum trees (Dipterocarpus alatus) up to the border with Lamphun Province. They were planted 130 years ago by the Prince of Chiang Mai.

Lamphun is a small town of spacious lawns. Its principal temple, **Wat Phra That Haripunchai**, founded in 1044 atop the site of a ruined royal palace, lies between the main street and the river. Although its entrance, guarded by two lions, faces the river on the eastern side, most visitors enter it through the western gate from the main street.

The first major structure you encounter is a stepped pyramidal chedi with niches containing standing Buddha images. You will note a resemblance with Chiang Mai's Chedi Liem and the chedi of nearby Wat Chamathewi of which this is a replica; there are several of similar design found throughout the North.

The dominant structure in the wide courtyard is a 50-m (164-ft) tall Lanna chedi covered in gold leaf. The original chedi was built in 1467; subsequent renovations raised it to its present height. Next to it is a viharn

Wat Phra That Haripunchai, chedi

Chiang Mai-Lamphun road

whose principal appeal is its lovely doors. Restored in 1925 after a fire, the viharn contains a fine bronze Chiang Saen Buddha image.

Wandering round the temple grounds you will see an impressive bronze gong hanging under a large bell. The bronze gong, northern Thailand's largest, was cast in 1860. The bell was cast four years later.

Exit from the eastern gate and cross the road and the footbridge over the Kwang River, a branch of the Ping River (in fact, the original channel before it shifted). This farming area holds **Wat Prayoon** with its Burmese-style chedi atop a former *mondop*, or square reliquary, built in 1369.

When sated, return to the wat, exit to the main street, turn left and walk to the corner. Cross the street to reach the **Lamphun National Museum**.

The small museum contains a fine collection of bronze images from

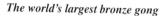
The world's largest bronze gong

Wat Phra That Haripunchai and surrounding temples. (Wednesday–Sunday 9am–4pm, except public holidays).

Walk or take a *samlor* down the street beside the museum to reach **Wat Chamathewi**, 1km (½ mile) to the west across the moat and past Wat Mahawan. The temple has a superb pair of unusual chedis, the larger of which has five tiers. Each tier has three niches and each niche holds a Buddha statue, making an impressive display of 15 Buddha images on each side or 60 on the four sides of the chedi.

Wat Chamathewi, also known as **Wat Kukut**, is named after its legendary 7th-century Mon queen founder, Chamathewi. Legend says that while pregnant, she left her husband for reasons unknown, heading north from Lavo (Lopburi) to find a new city. On the banks of the Kwang River, she gave birth to twin sons. Next, she ordered that a city protected by a rectangular moat be built. Called Haripunchai, this city's name was later changed to Lamphun.

The remains of that early period are found at Wat Chamathewi which, oddly, was built outside the protective confines of the city wall.

Two chedis, both renovated, stand next to the modern viharn: an octagonal stone chedi and a square, stepped pyramid on which the one in the Wat Phra That Haripunchai is modelled.

But it is the square chedi which commands one's attention: Here, standing stucco Buddha images, wearing tranquil expressions and diaphanous robes, watch over a wide, tree-lined courtyard.

Return to Chiang Mai by bus. These run every five minutes and the last one leaves at 7pm.

Motorcycle Jaunts

The beauty of a motorcycle is that it can take you to places cars cannot go. Despite the wealth of roads that have been constructed in the North, there are still lots of dirt tracks. They require a 125 c.c. trailbike and the skill to ride one. If you do not know how to ride a motorcycle, do not attempt to learn in Thailand. Slippery roads, dogs that dart across the highway, buffaloes and people that meander along it, and deep potholes all conspire to fuddle the unwary. If you are not confident of your riding ability, take the motorcycle on one of the other trips outlined here. There will still be plenty of challenges and you will be able to concentrate on the scenery instead of fighting the bike.

12. Baan Tawai

**Wat Chedi Liem, along the Ping River, through the countryside
to Baan Tawai, village of instant antiques. Trailbike or motorbike.**

Head south along the Chiang Mai-Lamphun Road. As you enter the
corridor of tall trees that line the sides of the road, you come to a
traffic light. About 1km (½ mile) past it is a 'Y' intersection; take
the right fork, marked by the sign: Ban Nong Hoi. About 1 km
farther on is **Wat Chedi Liem**.

Wat Chedi Liem, exemplifies one of the oldest stupa designs in
the kingdom. Similar to that in Lamphun's Wat Chamathewi, this
chedi was built by Chiang Mai's founder, King Mengrai, who must
have seen the original when he conquered Lamphun in 1281. He
built it in honour of his queen. She died in 1283 and King Mengrai
donated the chedi to the wat on its completion in 1288.

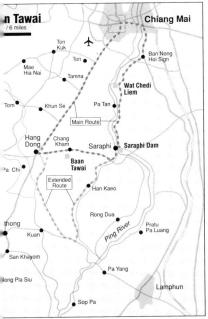

One kilometre (½ mile) farther
on, the road forks again at a big
banyan tree that stands before a
wat; take the right fork to
Saraphi Dam. On the left of the
dam is the river's original course
which passes Lamphun before
rejoining the Ping about 14km
(8¾ miles) south. Cross the dam
on the narrow iron bridge and at
the other side turn left. Continue
2km (1¼ miles) to a four-way
intersection. If you turn right
here, you will enter Baan Tawai
from the back.

To extend the journey, continue
straight at the intersection following the course of the Ping. The
route takes you down a dirt road
through pretty villages and gardens for 3km (1¾ miles), ending
at a T-junction. In the late afternoon, it is a lovely journey to turn
left and ride along the river, retracing your route when you feel

you have had enough. Otherwise, turn right at the 'T' junc-
tion and ride through fields for
another 2km (1¼ miles) or so to
Baan Tawai.

Baan Tawai is a village of
wood carvers who produce the
new antiques found in Chiang
Mai's shops. It little resembles a

Baan Tawai, wooden carvings

59

village these days, more a corridor of workshops whose goods are displayed in the yards. You can pick up some good bargains but getting a metre-tall wooden elephant home on your motorcycle is going to require a bit of ingenuity. There are several shippers in the village willing to help you, though.

Continue through Baan Tawai to **Hang Dong**. Turn right onto the Chiang Mai-Hot highway (H 108) and, a few kilometres later, arrive back in Chiang Mai. Along the way, browse at the ceramic shops found on either side of the road.

13. Back Country Biking

To Chom Thong, Mae Klang Waterfalls, Doi Inthanon and back via Mae Chaem, Ob Luang Gorge, and Hot.

Leave Chiang Mai on H 108, and head for Chom Thong 58km (36 miles) south. **Chom Thong** holds the handsome **Wat Phra That Si Chom Thong** with its beautiful gilded chedi that dates from 1451. The large cruciform viharn, built in 1516, also contains a collection of fine bronze images and

Excursions from Chiang Mai

25 miles / 40 km

Excursion 9
Excursion 13
Excursion 14
Excursion 18
Excursion 21

Mawkmai

B U R

2061

B U R M A

Mailun

Doi Khu
1332 ▲

Mae Lanna

Muang

Fish Cave

Lod Cave

Soppong

Pai

Mae Nam Pai

Mae Hong Son

Doi Ma
▲
2055

Nam Tok
Mae Surin

Nam Mae Chaem

Po Ka Nua

Khun Yuam

Doi Wi Cho Lo
1056

Doi Khun Bong
▲
1772

Nam Mae Yuam

Doi Inthanon
▲
2590

Mae Su

Sop Wak

Mae Chaem

Khao Om Phai
▲
1563

Om Meng

M
Kla
Fa

Mae Nam Salawi

Mae Sarieng

Pa Pong

Mae Sanam

Ob Luan

H

Buddha images carved on elephant tusks. Behind the principal Buddha is a small museum.

Have a drink at the restaurant next to the temple, then return to the head of the town and turn left onto the road to Doi Inthanon. seven km (4¼ miles) down on the left is the lovely **Mae Klang Waterfall**. At KM 8 is the entrance to the park. Just past it is the Visitor's Centre where you can buy a detailed map of the park and

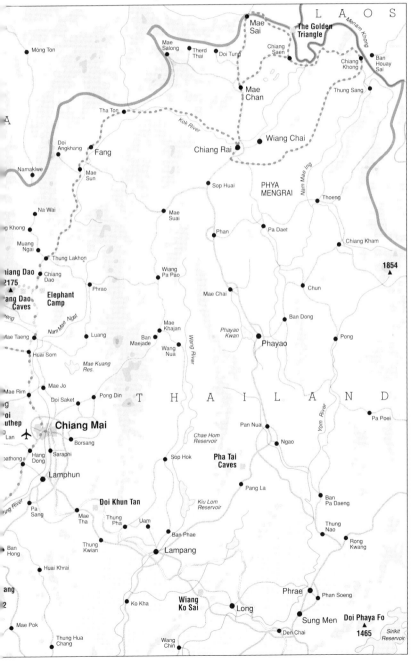

Mae Klang waterfalls

a birdwatching book that lists more than 360 species of birds sighted here.

The road then climbs through pine forests to the checkpost at KM 38 and then up a steep slope that is rain-shrouded during the monsoon season. At the 2,595m (8,514ft) summit at KM 49 there is a shrine to Chao Inthanon, a former prince of Chiang Mai, from whom the mountain received its name.

The views from the summit are somewhat disappointing, even in good weather. Start back down the mountain for the best viewpoint, which is at KM 40.8 by the two big, new chedis. At KM 38, just before the checkpoint, turn right onto H 1192. The one-lane road winds through some of the lushest, most beautiful forests in Thailand. Take your time both to enjoy the scenery and to negotiate the tight bends and steep descents.

The road opens into the Mae Chaem Valley and 22km (13¾ miles) later arrives at a 'Y' intersection. Take the right-hand fork into the town of **Mae Chaem** where you can have lunch.

To return to Chiang Mai, backtrack to the Y intersection 1 km before entering town and take the right fork on to H 1088. After 45km (28 miles) it reaches the main road (H 108) between Mae Sarieng and Hot. Turn left towards Hot, which is 22km (13¾ miles) away. A few kilometres on, you reach **Ob Luang Gorge**, billed as 'Thailand's Grand Canyon', a grand overstatement but worth a stop for a soft drink and a quick look. There is little to see in **Hot** but it does hold a motorcycle repair shop and gas station on the north end of town. After filling up, head north up H 108 and into Chiang Mai.

Wat Phra That Si Chom Thong, che

14. Back of Chiang Dao Mountain

A ride behind Thailand's third highest mountain on dirt roads. This trail is for experienced bikers only. Trailbike needed.

Just beyond the market in Chiang Dao (opposite the Shell station; fill up, you will need a full tank), a road to the left leads 5km (3 miles) past tobacco fields to the base of **Doi Chiang Dao**. Here, the road forks; go straight ahead to get to one of the more interesting **caves** of the north.

A hilltribe village

From there, back-track 100m (110yds) and take the right-hand fork. The dirt road crosses cotton fields shaded by tall gum trees (Diptocarpus alatus) and after a checkpost begins to climb. About 12km (7½ miles) up the road, a fork to the left will take you to **Baan Na Lao Mai**, a Lisu village behind of Doi Chiang Dao. Continue another 35km (21¾ miles) to the Karen village of Muang Khong on the banks of the Mae Taeng River. The route is steep and may be impassable after rainfall. The rewards, though, for persevering are beautiful forests and mountain scenery.

Caution For Motorcyclists

For some odd reason, travellers who have never ridden a motorcycle decide to learn during their stay in Chiang Mai, the worst possible training school. Traffic fatalities involving tourists are increasing and the sight of limping or bandaged foreigners in the streets of Chiang Mai is common.

Too much speed, sharp curves, the unstable gravel, mud or dust surfaces of many country roads, are the normal causes. Add dogs, cows, water buffalo, chickens, and people who do not look before crossing the road and you have a sure prescription for disaster for the unwary driver.

Protect yourself by renting a helmet (not all shops have them), wearing solid shoes, not sandals, and checking before you rent that the brakes, horn, lights and turn signals are in proper working order because you will need them all. Drive defensively by turning on your lights during the day when you see a car trying to overtake another in an on-coming lane.

Avoiding engine trouble: rental bikes are often not well-maintained but you should not compound the problem by using dirty or improper fuel. While the small petrol pumps along the road are picturesque, use them only in emergencies as the petrol they sell is often adulturated. It is better to fill up at an established petrol station. Contact Chiang Mai Motorcycle Touring Club (David Unkovich) at 21/1 Ratchmankhla Road, Soi 2 (053) 278-518. You can rent helmet, gloves and jacket there, also motorcycles, besides collecting maps and obtaining useful information and many hints that will help you plan your trip.

One further note: carry extra clothes since they will quickly soak up all the dirt and dust your wheels will kick up.

Flights

If pressed for time, fly rather than bus or drive to Chiang Rai and Mae Hong Son. Thai Airways offers two daily flights to Chiang Rai (40 minutes: Baht 420) and three or four flights daily to Mae Hong Son (40 minutes: Baht 345). There are also several flights between Bangkok and Chiang Rai.

15. Chiang Rai by Bicycle

Spend two fun days in Chiang Rai. Check into the Mae Kok Villa and rent a bicycle. There are many wats in Chiang Rai and you may be inspired to visit them all but only two rate close examination. The first is **Wat Phra Singh** on a short road that passes the central post office and links Singhalai and Uttarakit Roads.

The modern wat is distinguished by a fine pair of doors designed and carved by Thawan Duchanee, a local artist who became renowned in Bangkok and later in Germany. The doors are in his visceral style and the guardians are fierce enough to frighten away any demon. It says something about the liberality of the abbot that the guardians both have penises, one in the shape of a serpent and the other, an elephant's head.

The second temple is **Wat Phra Kaew** on Trairat Road between Ruang Nakhon and Singhalai Roads. A fine example of Lanna-style architecture, the viharn has lacquered doors and a carved wooden gable. The effect is marred only partially by the stained glass windows that form 'eyes' under the 'eyebrows'. The image inside is from the Chiang Saen period and probably dates from the 15th century.

Call in at the nearby **Tourist Authority of Thailand** offices at 448/16 Singhalai (Tel: 717-433), near the YMCA. A good map is available and information to help plan the rest of your visit. The network of roads in the town was laid out 100 years ago by Dr Briggs, a Canadian missionary. Unfortunately, he also pulled down the old walls that protected the inhabitants from their enemies.

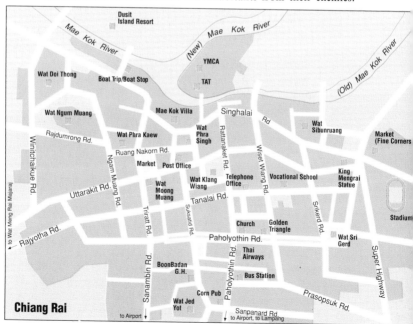

If you're looking for a longish bike ride, go upstream along the bank of the Mae Kok River beyond the **Dusit Island Resort**. At the base of Doi Tong cross the Mae Kah Luang Bridge and explore the countryside including a village close to a limestone peak. On the way back you might feel like having a swim in the Dusit Thani pool (Baht 150) or a snack in the coffee shop.

Wat Phra Singh, Chiang Rai

Spend the afternoon and evening contacting a trekking agency – and perhaps other travellers – to arrange a one-day tour to hilltribe villages for the following day. A visit to La Cantina might prove a good source of the latest information and gossip. Alternatives are the Bierstube, near the Wiang Inn, or the Silver Birch.

Chiang Rai city pillars

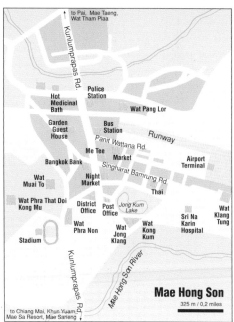

The map shows:

to Pai, Mae Taeng, Wat Tham Plaa

Kunlumprapas Rd.

Police Station
Hot Medicinal Bath
Wat Pang Lor
Garden Guest House
Bus Station
Panit Wattana Rd.
Runway
Me Tee
Market
Bangkok Bank
Singharat Bamrung Rd.
Airport Terminal
Wat Muai To
Night Market
Thai
Wat Phra That Doi Kong Mu
District Office
Post Office
Jong Kum Lake
Wat Phra Non
Wat Jong Klang
Wat Kong Kum
Sri Na Karin Hospital
Wat Klang Tung
Stadium
Kunlumprapas Rd.
Mae Hong Son River

Mae Hong Son
325 m / 0,2 miles

to Chiang Mai, Khun Yuam, Mae Sa Resort, Mae Sariang

16 . Mae Hong Son

Since a round-trip ticket from Chiang Mai costs so little, it is worth flying to Mae Hong Son even if it's for a day. There is a noticeable absence of public transportation in Mae Hong Son. When I asked a man how people got around town, he looked at me puzzled and said 'We walk' as if nothing could be more obvious. So start walking.

Lying in a valley, Mae Hong Son is also known as the 'Valley of Mists' because of its early morning fog and cloud-covered hills. The cold hard reality, though, is that Mae Hong Son lies on the border smuggling routes.

Once a quiet, peaceful province housing various ethnic groups including the Karen, Meo, Lawa, Shan, Lisu and Burmese, Mae Hong Son is also now suffused with hotels, guesthouses and trekking agencies catering to the tourist trade.

From the airport, take a minibus to your hotel. Find a hotel in the vicinity of the lake like the Piya Complex, the up-market Baiyoke Chalet, or one of the travellers guesthouses like Rose Garden, Jong Kum, or Fern House.

Depending on your flight, it will probably be early afternoon when you arrive. Spend some time just soaking up the atmosphere at **Jong Kum Lake**. There is a fitness park if you feel like working out. Visit the two Burmese-style wats that fringe the lake: **Wat Jong Klang** and **Wat Kong Kum**.

Both wats are fine examples of Burmese architecture with their tiny roofs stacked one atop the other and filigree woodwork along the eaves. The chedi, too, is a prime example of Burmese design with its terraced base, squat body, and spire of disks rising to a delicate crown representing a sacred umbrella shading a holy relic.

Wat Jong Klang has a fine collection of statues depicting scenes from the Vessantara Chadok, the last incarnation of the man

Wat Jong Klang, Mae Hong Son

who, in his next life would become the Buddha. Events in his life are also depicted in glass paintings.

In brief, the story is of a selfless monarch who is expelled from his kingdom for giving away a sacred white elephant. He subsequently hands his children to an old ascetic who demands their services as servants. When he is about to give away his wife, the gods intervene and, having proved his willingness to sacrifice everything, lead him back to the royal city where the inhabitants realize they have wronged him.

In the afternoon, walk to **Wat Phra Non** and its 12-m (31-ft) long **Reclining Buddha** image, the position the Buddha

Wat Jong Klang – worshipper

assumed when he died. Cross the street and brace yourself; you are about to climb a stairway as difficult as that which ascends Chiang Mai's Doi Suthep. It leads to **Wat Phra That Doi Kong Mu**. There is a road if you can find transportation.

The wat comprises two beautiful chedis and a commanding view of the surrounding countryside. Walk to the parapet on the eastern

Pa Dawn woman

rim to watch the sun set over the town and the mountains. Few views are as impressive as this.

Descend the stairs. For dinner, walk to the **night market** on Kunlumprapas Road and order Thai food from the stalls.

After dinner, walk to the **Cathay movie theatre** and watch a Thai movie which begins at 7.30pm. Before returning to your hotel, stroll down to the lake to enjoy the tiny lights on the Wat Jong Klang chedi as they reflect in the water.

The next morning, rise early to watch sunrise and see why Mae Hong Son is also called the 'Valley of Mists'. Rise before dawn and walk to the lake's edge to watch the chedi's reflection on the shimmering water and the barefoot monks in their saffron robes padding along on their morning alms walk.

Then, watch the sun melt away the fog and reveal the wat in its full beauty. Take a short walk to the nearby market for breakfast before going on with the rest of the tour.

Hire a bahtbus to the boat landing about 6km (3¾ miles) south of town past the Mae Hong Son Resort. There, you can bargain with a boatman to take you to the village of **Huay Poo Gaeng** near the Burmese border to visit the Pa Dawn or Karen (the so-called 'long-necked' people) whose women are famous for wearing heavy brass rings around their necks. This gives them the appearance of having long necks. In fact, the rings do not stretch the neck but depress the collarbones.

In the afternoon, hire a bahtbus (or catch the bus to Pai) to go to **Wat Tham Plaa**, 17km (10½ miles) up H 1095 towards Pai. Turn left at a sign that says '**Fish Cave**' and go 200m (218yds) to a narrow suspension bridge. Cross it and five minutes later arrive at the cave. Next to it is a pool bubbling from a subterranean stream. The pool holds fish up to 1 metre (3.3 ft) long which you can feed with bread bought at the park official's hut.

Return to Mae Hong Son and spend the early evening shopping for Burmese *kalaga* tapestries, lacquerware, and cloth on **Singharat Bamrung Road**; the La-or Shop has a wide selection.

Dine at the **Fern Restaurant**, just downhill from the Post Office. The restaurant is run by former graduates of Chulalongkorn University and serves excellent Thai food.

The next morning, fly back to Chiang Mai.

Note: Visitors who intend to travel to and from Mae Hong Son by air should be aware that departures can be disrupted by rain and heavy mists.

If you are on a tight schedule, you should keep this in mind. If you need to return to Chiang Mai by road, the journey may take between 6–8 hours.

Yao hilltribe women

17. Hilltribe Treks

Once again, I voice my reservations about hilltribe treks. When they were first offered a decade ago, few people went on them so they made little impact on the villages and their cultures. Today, there are dozens of companies and they are making serious inroads, irrevocably changing the cultures, creating a false economy and contributing little of lasting value.

If you wish to take a trek, minimise the adverse effects by ensuring you sign on with a reputable trekking agency. There are dozens of companies and trying to recommend one over another is difficult as the quality of the trek is dependent as much on the guide as on the provisions, and the guides frequently change companies. Shop around; ask some serious questions to determine whether the proprietors are merely cashing in on a popular moneymaker or are they sensitive to tribal customs and seeking to make the minimum impact.

Ask about the size of your trekking group. A group of more than six persons tends to take over a small village. Try to find a trek that visits one or two tribal groups only, not skipping through one village after another in rapid succession. Find an agency that employs hilltribesmen as guides. There is some antipathy between the tribes and Thai guides and there have been accusations of cultural insensitivity. If your would-be guide seems to understand nothing of the culture, find another agency. There are trekking companies along Tha Phae Road and Chaiyaphum Road. One, on Charoen Prathet Road, makes the painful offer: 'Visit Elephant Riding on Foot'.

MOONSHINE TOUR & TREKKING

Popular trekking areas are due north of Chiang Mai, between Chiang Dao and Mae Salong, and the hills around Chiang Rai. Some treks combine village visits with elephant rides and short river runs on bamboo rafts.

While on these trips, dress casually but adequately to protect your skin from the burning sun. I have seen Western women sitting topless on a raft on a sunny day.

This is not only insensitive but it is also asking for trouble. Males, too, should be able to withstand the heat without stripping down to their shorts.

Passengers meet Akha trinket sellers

Jogging or walking shoes are sufficient for hilltribe trekking. Some agencies provide sleeping bags and mosquito nets; others require you to take your own. Check with the agency before making a booking. Carry a daypack with a change of clothes (two, if during the rainy season) wrapped in plastic bags. Carry a canteen rather than plastic water bottles which often get discarded, creating an environmental problem. Puritabs, available in most pharmacies, will purify the water. Canteens, ponchos, sleeping bags and other equipment are sold in shops along Manee Noparat Road near the northeast corner of the city wall.

Malaria is prevalent in the hills. The best medical advice is: Don't put your faith in anti-malarial pills. Avoid being bitten by mosquitoes and use plenty of repellent and a mosquito net. See a doctor and do not accept flu as a diagnosis if you develop a fever after you return from your trek. Insist on a blood test and mention malaria to your doctor. Do not delay.

Chiang Mai can be surprisingly dry during the winter months and it is advisable to carry chapstick and moisturiser.

Last but not least, carry toilet paper along with you.

Lahu children on balcony

18. Golden Triangle by Water

Down the Kok River to Chiang Rai (night), drive to Mae Sai and the Golden Triangle (night), drive to Chiang Saen and Chiang Rai (night). By local bus and rented car. Alternatively, ride a motorcycle to Tha Thon and have the boatmen ferry it to Chiang Rai. This excursion takes 3½ days.

Catch the 6am or 7.20am bus from the Chang Pheuak Bus Station on a four-hour journey to **Tha Thon**. If you ride a motor-cycle, you can leave at 8am and still have time for the 9am show at the **Chiang Dao Elephant Camp** at KM 56.

The road climbs out of the val-ley and along the beautiful Ping River. Past Chiang Dao, it runs through tall teak forests before entering the plains around Fang and from there to Tha Thon.

On reaching the large bridge over the Mae Kok River, turn right and you will see boats tied up to the bank. Boats leave for Chiang Rai for a set hire fee of 1,600 baht per boat, carrying up to eight passengers. Try to leave by 2pm. The four-hour journey down the Kok River to Chiang Rai takes you past hilltribe villages and grass-lands. As it is a valley, there is little spectacular scenery or whitewater.

Spend the afternoon exploring **Chiang Rai** by bicycle (see Excursions) and then stay the night. The next morning, rent a car for two days and head to **Mae Sai**.

Some 870km (540 miles) from Bangkok, Mae Sai is the north-ernmost point in Thailand. After passing rows of shophouses, the road ends at the **Sai River Bridge**. For some decades now the town has prospered, bartering all kinds of goods from Burmese jade, antiques to commodities. Mae Sai is a good place to look for these items. The border, closed except to locals for almost 40 years, is now open to a limited extent to foreign visitors, Monday to Friday, 8am–6pm. You need your passport, plus a photo-copy and US$10. The Thai immigration office will issue a laissez faire pass (There is no charge, the US$10 in cash is paid to the Burmese officials).

Boat ride down Kok River

71

Boats for trips up the Mekong River

Stay in a hotel here or, if you have made reservations, in the **Golden Triangle Hotel**. To reach the Golden Triangle, drive back down H 110 for about 300m (330yds) and turn left next to the Sin Wattana Hotel onto a paved road. It is 28km (17½ miles) to the Golden Triangle Hotel on the banks of the Mekong River. If this is too fancy for you, there are guesthouses farther along the road.

In the morning, take breakfast at the arch that demarcates the Golden Triangle and marvel at the fact that were there not a sign-post, there would be nothing to hold your interest, so ordinary is the landscape. The site marks the juncture of the borders of Thailand, Myanmar and Laos and that is about it.

Rent a boat for a 25-minute cruise around the principal island in the Mekong or pay slightly more to continue downriver to Chiang Saen. Catch a bahtbus for the 9-km journey back to the Golden Triangle arch to pick up your car.

Chiang Saen is one of the prettiest towns in the North principally because the city fathers have resisted the urge to modernise the town and cut down all its trees. Set on the banks of the Mekong, it is an important archaeological site, holding more than 130 ruins. The present city, thought to date from 1328, is built atop the ruins of an earlier settlement.

Drive down the road leading at right angles from the river towards Chiang Rai. Within a few hundred metres, are the ruins of the city wall. Stop to examine it and the moat that was once filled by the waters of the Mekong. Just past the wall, turn right down a dirt road to **Wat Pasak**.

Pasak means 'teak forest' and while many of the trees are gone, those that remain give a particularly bucolic atmosphere to the site. The brick chedi, built in 1295, has been restored, robbing it of some of its antique flavour but the faces of the stucco Buddhas in the niches reflect the tranquil air of the original.

More impressive is the hilltop **Wat Phra That Chom Kitti** down the same dirt road. At its base are the three broken chedis of Wat Chom Chang. Climb the moss-covered stairway to the 25-m (82-ft) chedi, covered in copper plates.

Return to the highway and re-enter the city walls. In ages past, the first impressive monument you would have seen is **Wat Chedi Luang**, a 58-metre (190-ft) high octagonal chedi built in 1331 amidst teak trees. Next door is the **Chiang Saen Museum**, (Daily 9am–4pm, except Mondays, Tuesdays and official holidays.) which houses a fine collection of Chiang Saen bronze Buddha images and other artifacts.

Wat Pasak, Chiang Saen

Wander through the back streets to find other chedis and ruins sitting next to wooden houses. There are some superb photographic opportunities here. Drive back to the river and turn right, exiting the town on H 1129. At KM 49, turn right and climb the hill on which **Wat Phra That Pha Ngao** is situated. Beside the rather ordinary chedi is a steel tower. Climb it for a magnificent view of the Mekong River and the Laotian countryside.

There are now two all-weather roads to Chiang Khong, 53km (33 miles) away on the Mekong River. The lower route has good views of the river, whilst the other route goes near hilltribe villages. Accommodation in Chiang Khong is available at **Ban Golden Triangle**, a five-room, Thai-style house. Contact housekeeper Khun Malika, Tel: 791-350 for reservations.

Buses leave from the Chiang Rai bus station every hour for the 3½-hour journey to Chiang Mai. There are air-conditioned buses at 8, 9, and 11am. If you are driving, take H 1020 and H 1152 via Phya Mengrai.

View of the Mekong

Whitewater rafting down the Pai River

19. Pai River Rafting

A 2–3 days river rafting trip through wildlife sanctuary.

Between 1st July and 31st December, the Thai Adventure Co Ltd (Tel: 699-111; Manager: Guy Gorias) operates interesting and exciting two to three days whitewater rafting trips down the Pai River through wild countryside.

On the first day, you will be driven 64km (39¾ miles) to a branch of the Pai River. There, you board rubber rafts and paddle through wildlife sanctuary, lunch and stopping for a swim. You make another short afternoon trip before setting up camp, cooking dinner and settling down for the night.

The next morning you walk to the **Wind Cave**. After lunch, you'll raft to Pai River with its Class 2-3 rapids (Class 6 is the most difficult) and hot springs. Camp overnight by a freshwater stream in the forest.

Day three takes you rafting through the **Pai Canyon** and four more rapids, ending at the Mae Hong Son Valley at about 2pm. Lunch is served there. You'll be transferred back to Mae Hong Son.

This 50-km trip can be done in two days by omitting the walk to Wind Cave. Cost of the trip, including food and all equipment, is 1,500 baht for two days and 2,000 baht for three days. Thai Adventure Co Ltd is located at **Chez Swan Restaurant** on Pai's main street, Rungaiyanon Road. This restaurant is highly recommended for its French and Thai cuisine.

By bamboo raft down river

20. Kok River Float

Down the Kok River on a bamboo raft. A 3-day trip.

Float leisurely down the Kok River from **Tha Thon** to **Chiang Rai** on a bamboo raft that holds up to eight persons. You take turns steering the vessel through the calmer portions of the river. The first night is spent in a hilltribe village, and the second around a campfire in the open countryside.

The price depends on how fancy you want your food arrangements to be. Arrange it with the friendly Thip at Thip's Travellers House and Restaurant at Tha Thon. Tel: 245-538. To reach Tha Thon from Chiang Mai, see Excursion 18.

21. Shan and Lahu Village Visits

Pai (night), Mae Hong Son (2 nights), Mae Sarieng, Ob Luang Gorge. Local bus but more comfortable by jeep. 4-5 days.

Orange bus No. 612 departs from the Chiang Mai Arcade Bus Station (Platform 9) at two-hourly intervals from 7am to 2.30pm for the 135km (84 miles) four-hour trip to Pai. If you are driving or motorcycling, head north on H 107 towards Mae Taeng (KM 36), turn left onto H 1095.

For those who believe that flying down a country road blows the city out of your pores, this is your journey. The drive is along a twisted, paved road that climbs ridges and threads valleys, through superb mountain scenery studded with small hamlets.

It finally enters a broad valley and the small town of **Pai** which lies on the banks of the **Pai River** and has the air of an alpine village. Small hotels line the main street, the best known being Pai in the Sky. Spend the day enjoying its peace.

Rent a bicycle near the bus station or walk to the base of the hill near **Wat Mae Yen** (the Temple on the Hill) to the east. Continue past the temple to visit **Shan villages**, eventually intersecting with the main road. Just past the wooden bridge is a turn to the right that takes you along the river through three more Shan villages on a 4.7 km loop that will bring you back to the highway and into Pai itself. The Shans, also known as *Thai Yai* (Great Thais) are believed to have migrated from China's Yunnan province, down rivers and streams into the upper valleys of the Southeast Asian river system in

Streets of Pai

Wat Boonruang, Mae Sarieng

the 10th century. Many settled in Upper Burma, others went on to parts of Thailand such as Pai.

There are other walks and rides to the west of town. Head past the Pai Hospital on a 7km (4¼ miles) journey that will take you past Shan, KMT Chinese refugee, and Lahu villages to end at a pretty waterfall. The road is better suited to feet than to bicycles but with perseverance you can make the ride.

Call in on Guy Gorias of Thai Adventure Co Ltd to ask about the possibility of trips by rubber raft or canoe down the Pai River (see Excursion 19). His office is at Chez Swan Restaurant on the main road.

Buses leave Pai at 7, 9, and 11am and 1.30pm for the 109km (67.7 miles) journey to Mae Hong Son. The scenery is more rugged, with long narrow valleys and pine-topped ridges that look into deep valleys. In portions, the road is not yet paved but is passable. The bus arrives in **Mae Hong Son** four hours later. For details of how to spend two days in the town, see Excursion 12.

From Mae Hong Son, it is 350km (217.4 miles) back to Chiang Mai by the southern route. Buses depart the station at 6 and 8am and 12.30, 8 and 9pm for the 8-hour journey through hills and

15 Spots For Perfect Postcard Shots

Chiang Mai
1. Doi Suthep
2. Chiang Mai-Lamphun Highway
3. Muang Mai market
4. Wat Suan Dok
5. Nawarat Bridge
6. Wat Chedi Liem
7. Doi Pui
8. Buak Hat Park and Flower Market

Elsewhere
1. The road between Pai and Mae Hong Son
2. Hill overlooking Mae Hong Son
3. Hilltribe villages
4. Mae Salong streets
5. The bridge into Myanmar at Mae Sai
6. Chiang Saen (almost anywhere)
7. Wat Phra That Lampang Luang in Lampang

Photo Info

While Thais will generally pose for photos without your asking, you will find that in a hilltribe village, the click of a shutter triggers the automatic extension of a hand and a demand for money. To avoid a ruckus, pay a baht or two. For children, you may get off with a piece of candy; carry a small bagful.

Major brands print and slide films are available in Chiang Mai and Chiang Rai. Check that the expiration date stamped on the side of the box has not passed and that the shop's film display case is not exposed to the sun. Shops in Chiang Mai, Lampang and Chiang Rai can process print film and print photos in as little as 23 minutes.

narrow, rice-terraced valleys. Break your journey in **Mae Sarieng**, four hours down the road. Mae Sarieng offers fine views along its river and two wats, one behind the other. The first, **Wat Uttayarom**, is undistinguished, but the second, **Wat Boonruang**, has the multi-tiered roofs and wooden lacework one associates with east coast American shore homes built in the 1890s.

From Mae Sarieng, the road heads due east. Along the way are several rest stops: look out for signs with a tree falling on a picnic table.

At KM 17 is **Ob Luang National Park** (Thailand's mini-version of the Grand Canyon) where a fast-flowing river pours through a narrow gap.

H 1088 rejoins H 108 at **Hot**, little more than a wide spot in the road. The bus continues through **Chom Thong** with its lovely **Wat Phra That Si Chom Thong** (see Excursion 13) and brings you back to Chiang Mai.

The following are unscheduled events. If you happen upon them, stop to observe.

Planting or harvesting rice.

Elephants working in forests. Rarer since the logging ban but still possible to see in the areas around Chiang Dao and Mae Hong Son.

Fishermen tossing their circular nets in the countryside and on the moat around the city wall.

Flocks of ducks and their tenders. If you see the ground moving ahead of you it is probably a closely-packed collection of ducks "out for a walk".

Cock fights. Near Ban Nong Hoi south of Chiang Mai and in villages.

Men playing *maak ruuk*, a vigorous, Thai form of chess enjoyed when the sun is high.

Takraw. The game where a rattan ball is propelled by every extremity but the hands through a hoop or over a net.

Countryside funerals are marked by long processions along the roads to a cremation tower in the fields. You are welcome to join.

Rocket festivals. Normally associated with the Northeast, villages in the north fire homemade bamboo rockets into the May sky to induce the gods to shower their rice fields and ensure bountiful harvests.

Special events

Temple fairs. During the winter months, Buddhists hold fairs to raise money for temple repairs. There is a festive atmosphere with carnival rides and produce stalls. If the roof needs repair, the monks will sell tiles and the donor's name will be written on the obverse side before it is set in place. You are welcome to contribute.

Eating Out

As elsewhere in Thailand, one of the pleasures of a Chiang Mai visit is the chance to dine on fine food. Cuisines range from Thai, which is rapidly gaining popularity in the West, to Continental and Asian. Best of all, the prices are quite reasonable.

One of the attractions of dining in Chiang Mai is the lovely settings of its restaurants: old Lanna homes, riverside inns, and gardens ensure a different experience every evening.

A Taste of Thailand

Thai dishes are as individual and as varied as the chefs who prepare them. Thai cooks rely on garlic, lemon grass, chillis, coriander, fish paste and dozens of herbs and spices to impart an astounding variety of delicious flavours to their dishes. Although most are spicy, they can be cooked more blandly on request. Among the fiery favourites are *Thom Yam Gung* (piquant soup with shrimp), *Gaeng Khiew Wan Gai* (A hot green curry with chicken or beef), and *Gaeng Phet* (a red curry with beef).

Thai desserts often contain coconut

Tossing Som-dtam, a Thai-style salad

Non-spicy dishes include: *Thom Kha Gai* (coconut milk curry with chicken), *Plaamuk Thawd Krathiem Prik Thai* (squid fried with garlic and black pepper; also made with fish), *Nua Phat Namman Hoi* (beef in oyster sauce), *Muu Phat Priew Wan* (sweet and sour pork), and *Homok Talay* (a seafood mousse; it can be made spicy). And then there is Chiang Mai's own cuisine whose key dishes are listed below.

Note: The very practical Thais eat with a fork in the left hand and spoon in the right, using the fork to guide the food onto the spoon which then transports it to the mouth.

Desserts

Desserts are a Thai speciality. Try coconut ice cream (ice cream *kathit*) and a host of goodies with a base of coconut milk or vermicelli and incorporating sticky rice and luscious fruits. You can literally munch your way down a street and not repeat a taste.

Thai durian

The traditional Thai meal-ender (and the perfect counter to the spiciness of the dishes and the heat of the night) is a simple plate of fruit, usually papaya, pineapple and watermelon, peeled and cut

Northern Cuisine

Khao New. Northern food is generally eaten with *Khao New* or sticky rice. One kneads a bit of rice into a ball and dips it in the various sauces and curries.

Sai Oua. A chewy, oily, spicy pork sausage also called *nam* and associated with the North. It is roasted over a fire fuelled by coconut husks which impart an aroma to the meat. Although normally prepared hygienically, it is best to buy it only at better restaurants. Beware the buried *prik kii nuu* chillies that present the unwary with a painful surprise.

Khao Soy. Originally a Burmese speciality, this egg noodle dish is filled with chunks of beef or chicken, lightly curried in a gravy of coconut cream, and sprinkled with crispy noodles and garlic.

Nam Prik Ong. Minced pork, chillies, tomatoes, garlic and shrimp paste are blended and cooled. It is served with crisp cucumber slices, parboiled cabbage leaves and crispy pork rind (the latter is another northern snack).

Larb. A minced pork, chicken, beef, and even fish dish. It is associated with Northeastern cuisine where it is normally eaten raw; *larb* in the North, however, is thoroughly cooked. It is served with long beans, mint leaves, cabbage, and other raw vegetables which contrast with its full-bodied meaty flavour.

Gaeng Hang Lay. Also derived from Burma, and one of the spiciest of northern dishes, it should be approached with caution by those with tender palates. Pork and tamarind flesh give this curry a sweet and sour flavour. The curry is especially suitable as a dip for a ball of sticky rice.

Mieng is a Burmese delicacy of fermented tea leaves that tastes a lot better than it sounds.

Khantoke dinner. This buffet of northern dishes provides an excellent introduction to Northern cuisine. Lest you think it is served only to tourists, wander through a morning market and see steaming pots of its key dishes set out for customers.

A typical Khantoke dinner includes seven main dishes: *Khaeng Hanglae* (pork curry with garlic and ginger), *Naam Prik Ong kab Khaeb Muu* (minced pork with tomato and chili paste), pork crackling, *larb* (minced pork, chicken, fish or beef); and *Sai Oua* (spicy northern pork sausage)

into bite-sized chunks. Vary it with banana, tangerine and seasonal fruits like jackfruit, rambutan, mangoes, and mangosteen. If you crave a taste treat akin to a gourmet Limburger cheese, bite into a durian.

Patongkoh

Drinks

For a refreshing drink, try a shake made of pureed fruit, crushed ice and a light syrup. Chilled young coconuts are delicious: drink the juice, then scrape out and eat the tender young flesh. Soft drinks like Coca-Cola are found everywhere. Try Vitamilk, a refreshing drink made from soybeans. For a revitalising cooler, order a bottle of soda, a glass of ice and a sliced lime. Squeeze the lime into the glass, add the soda and your thirst is slaked.

Sip the very strong Thai coffee bolstered with chicory or tamarind. The odd orange Thai tea is sticky sweet but delicious. On a hot day, Chinese drink a hot, very thin tea, believing that ice is bad for the stomach but the truth is that all three taste great over ice.

Local beers include Singha, Amarit and Kloster. The best local whisky since 1939 is called Mekhong, distilled from glutinous rice and usually bought by the half-bottle. Best drunk with plenty of soda, ice and – very important – a squeeze of lime. Most foreign liquors are available. Large restaurants have wine lists.

Restaurants

Thai

For a Thai-style breakfast, wander into the side streets by the **Ton Lamyai Market**. Sidewalk vendors will be deep-frying the tasty X-

shaped pastries called *patongkoh*. Order them with the very thick but tasty Thai coffee which is served with a layer of condensed milk in the bottom. Insist on *Cafe Thai* or you will be served Nescafe which, while delicious, lacks the punch of the Thai variety. So thick is it, it is served with a tea chaser. In the listings below, unless otherwise stated, the restaurants are found in Chiang Mai. For restaurants outside Chiang Mai, check the addresses following the names of the restaurant to find out if they are in Chiang Rai or Mae Hong Son.

Ma-Prang (Star Fruit), at 25 Charoen Prathet Road across from Pornping Hotel, serves Thai food under the spreading branches of tall trees. Try its Roast Chicken Northern Style with basil leaves which is served in a light broth. Try also the Northern Spicy Sausage (*nam*), fried morning-glory, and Pork Curry Burmese Style. Very economical prices.

Krua Khun Phan, 80/1 Intrawarorot Road (near Suan Dok Gate) is one of several Thai restaurants behind Wat Phra Singh. Its appeal lies in its displays of ready-made Thai dishes and in the Thai-house atmosphere of its dining hall.

Bain's Garden, 2/2 Wat Ket Road, Soi 1, is in the compound owned many years ago by the forestry department of the Borneo Co Ltd. It provides the diner a superb view of the gardens while he samples a variety of economically-priced Thai dishes. Not fancy but nice. Daily 10am–9pm.

Khantoke dinners are a good way to combine Northern Thai cuisine with Lanna culture. Some visitors will find the Cultural Shows touristy, especially the hilltribe segments. For the price, however, they are worth an evening's attendance.

The Diamond Riverside Hotel on Charoen Prathet Road. Lanna *Khantoke* dinner at 7pm followed by classical Lanna and hilltribe dancing. Tel: 270-080 for reservations.

The Old Chiang Mai Cultural Centre at 185/3 Wua Lai Road offers a similar programme with a *Khantoke*-style dinner beginning at 7pm followed by a cultural show in a large hall and a hilltribe presentation outside. The whole programme ends at about 10pm. Call 274-093 or 274-540 for reservations.

Khrua Sabai, at the golf driving range opposite Airport Plaza. Tel: 274-042. Its Thai-Chinese food is highly recommended.

Aroon-Rai at 46 Kotchsarn Road (Tel: 276-947) has been established for decades. Ambassadors and ministers of state have had meals here, praising its tasty Thai and Northern Thai dishes.

82

Riverside Restaurant (9-11 Charoen Rat Road opposite Chinda Hospital) has been for some years a popular meeting place for visitors in the evening. Under Thai/Dutch management. If you are looking for a quiet dinner, go elsewhere. If you want a cheerful, convivial atmosphere this is it. Overlooking the Ping River, it serves excellent meals and offers a host of live bands playing middle-of-the-road classics. Tel: 243-239.

Kai Wan at 181 Nimmanahaeminda Road. Wooden Thai house in pleasant garden, lunch in open-sided room under the house, dinner on the balcony upstairs. Popular with residents as well as visitors. Lunch and dinner at reasonable prices. Tel: 222-147.

Riverfront restaurant

Grilled Chicken with Honey is both the name and the primary dish in this unpretentious restaurant on Charoen Prathet Road next to Pornping Hotel. It serves Northeastern food with *larb* and other favourites. Daily 8pm–10pm.

Ruang Thong at 742/1 Paholyothin Road, Chiang Rai. For reservations or other queries, call Tel: 712-677.

Golden Triangle Restaurant, 590 Paholyothin Road, Chiang Rai. Tel: 711-339. Lunch and dinner too.

Haw Nalika, 302/1-2 Paholyothin Road, Chiang Rai, not far from the Clock Tower in the main street. A favourite eating place for all. Tel: 711-373.

Khai Mook (Pearl), 71 Khunlumpraphat Road, Mae Hong Son. Tel: 612-092. Thai cusine.

Fern Restaurant, just downhill from the Post Office in Mae Hong Son, run by former graduates of Chulalongkorn University and serving excellent Thai food. The chicken legs soup with coconut cream makes a meal here memorable.

Vegetarian

Whole Earth, 88 Sri Don Chai Road. Tel: 282-463. This Thai vegetarian restaurant in Chiang Mai serves both Thai vegetarian and non-vegetarian dishes in a garden setting. Recommended dishes are: Aloo gobi (cauliflower, potatoes with Indian curry), Vietnamese spring rolls, Thai curry with tofu, egg-plant in coconut milk, Smoothie (fresh fruit in honey and yoghourt).

Naina, 128 Charoen Rat Road, serves Indian vegetarian food.

Restaurants with Live Music

Teejays Tavern at 1 Changlor Road (200m west of Chiang Mai Gate). Australian management, matey. Good grub and generous helpings, as one would expect. Occasional live music and sometimes crowded. Closed on Sunday. Tel: 271-950.

Brasserie Restaurant & Bar at 37 Chareon Rat Road (beyond Chinda Hospital). Live music nightly. A current favourite for late night music and refeshments. Tel: 241-665.

Riverside Restaurant at 9-11 Chareon Rat Road (see also Thai Food listing) has a Thai-Dutch management. Several live bands play here and the restaurant has been popular since its opening years ago.

Game

Kai Tong Restaurant: Beasts of the jungle, live for your selection. The range includes rabbit, cobra, deer, eels, frogs, soft-shelled tortoises, monitor lizards, crocodiles, and others. Its speciality is python steak and Barking Deer, a protected species. If you can bring yourself to order the beasts after looking at them in their tiny cages, then you have more guts than I do. Located at 67 Kotchasan Road. Daily 10am–1am. Tel: 236-584.

International

Daret's at 4/5 Chaiyaphum Road is an outdoor restaurant where budget travellers gather. Despite the low prices, the food is quite good. Try Chicken Cordon Bleu and fruit shakes. Come here if you crave a Banana Split. A good place to meet and watch people.

English

The Pub. Huai Kaeo Road near the Amari Rincome Hotel. Tel: 211-550. Superb English meals in a homely atmosphere; in the winter, logs blaze in the living room fireplace. The Pub, located in a house with a quiet garden, has been serving excellent English fare for decades.

French

Le Coq d'Or, 68/1 Koh Klang, Nong Hoi. Established for 21 years, this French restaurant is a favourite of both Thai and foreign dignitaries and 'people who matter'. The restaurant is located in an old house which is a bit inconvenient to get to but, nevertheless, worth a try. Tel: 282-024.

German

Bier Stube, 33/6A Moonmuang Road, Chiang Mai, Tel: 210-869. Near Tha Pae Gate. Good, standard German fare.

Haus Munchen, 115/3 Loi Kroh Road, diagonally opposite Novotel Hotel. Tel: 274-027.

Bierstube, Paholyothin Road, Chiang Rai. German fare. Near the Wiang Inn. Run by the owner, Karl Heinz.

Italian

Pensione La Villa, 145 Rajdamnoen Road, Tel: 277-403. Italian dishes in a garden setting.

Babylon, 100/63 Huai Kaeo Road, opposite the entrance to Chiang Mai University, specialises in pizza and a variety of Italian dishes. Open 11am–2pm, 6pm–10pm. Tel: 212-180.

Japanese

Musashi, 53/6 Inthawarorot Road, Tel: 210-944. Favoured by Japanese food aficionados.

Market Munching

Besides eating at the inexpensive and fine restaurant in Chiang Mai, you should also try the delicious Thai fare at market and street stalls where the Thais shop.

It is great fun to wander from stall to stall in the Anusarn Market that begins across from Royal Princess Hotel on Chang Khlan Road and ends on Charoen Prathet Road. Here, you will find stalls with names like **Number One Cock Fire**, and **Fatty Fatty**, each specialising in a different dish.

Try a dish at one stall and then move on to another. Among the many possibilities are Honey Chicken (Chicken basted in honey and roasted over an open fire), *Guay Tiew Phat Thai* (fried noodles with bits of shrimp, pork and bean sprouts), and *Khai Jiew Hoy* (eggs scrambled with a generous serving of mussels.

Don't miss 'Morning-Glory Flying', a concept that originated in Pattaya. The chef cooks a batch of delicious morning-glory plants in his wok. When it is finished, he heaves it high in the air and a waiter standing next to the patron's table catches it in a plate which he sets before the diner. The original Fast Food.

In Mae Hong Son, an early morning bowl of *Khao thom*, rice gruel with bits of pork and other flavourings, makes a great start to any day.

A feast for both the palate and the eyes

Nightlife

Nightlife in Chiang Mai was undreamt of 30 years ago. All the same, the Blue Moon started up then in a subdued way and is still in business with a large band and an array of singers. The larger hotels run to discos. Alongside the moat, near the Tha Phae Gate, are a variety of bars, some with live music, some with taped music and videos, some with music and hostesses. A Bangkok-style bar has opened with go-go girls. Not to be outdone, there are now bars for gays as well.

With AIDS on the rise, take prophylactic precautions, as you would anywhere else in the world. It would be foolish and death-defying not to do so.

But nightlife in Chiang Mai is not necessarily seamy. In fact, the northern city is much more subdued than its sister city, Bangkok. For many visitors to Chiang Mai, nightlife would consist of shopping or eating out at the night markets in Chang Khlan Road.

Bars with Hostesses
Blue Moon, 5/3 Moon Muang Road. Tel: 214-818. Typical large Thai-style night club, attractive hostesses, worth a visit.

Music Bars
Among the most popular are **Old West** on Huai Kaeo Road, and

Early Times and **Captain Hook's** on Kotchasan Road. **Baritone** at 96 Post office Road presents jazz nightly at 9pm.

Gay Bars

The Butterfly Room at 126 Loi Khroa Road is open from 11am–2am. There is also a cabaret show. Tel: 249-315.

The Coffee Boy at 248 Toonghotel Road is in an old Thai Lanna teak house. Classical music in a peaceful setting. Be forewarned, though, that this bar is located in a seedy side of town. Open 8pm–2am; with special shows on Friday, Saturday and Sunday, from 11pm. Tel: 244-458.

Massages

Both traditional (also called 'Ancient') and non-traditional massages are offered. In the former, you are led to a comfortable room and massaged by a masseuse chosen by the management. In the latter, you pick your masseuse from behind a one-way mirror. She bathes you, massages you and whatever else you do, the two of you decide. The fee to the parlour is set; that for the extra services is determined by discussion between you and the masseuse.

Diamond Riverside Hotel, 33/10 Chareon Prathet Road. Tel: 270-081. (*Traditional*)

Northern Blind School at the corner of Arak Street and Soi 1, Inthawarorot Road near Suan Dok Gate. Tel: 221-009. (*Traditional*)

Rinkaew Phovech, 183/4 Wua Lai Road, beside the Old Chiang Mai Cultural Centre. Tel: 274-565, Daily 8am–8pm. (*Traditional*)

Saiyuri. Soi 2, Bamrung Rat Road. Tel: 242-361. (*non-traditional*)

Cinemas

Vista Hotel, near the railway station, has two cinemas, Vista One and Two. There is also another Vista cinema at the Central Department Store Complex on Huai Kaeo Road. **Mahanakorn Theatre** near the Chang Pheuak Gate on the highway north shows Thai movies that run the gamut from tragedy to comedy, all within 100 or so minutes. That they are in Thai language should not deter you. Sit back and let them carry you away.

Discos

The Plaza. Chiang Mai Plaza Hotel.

The Wall. Chiang Inn Hotel.

Chiang Rai

La Cantina, 528/20 Bunphaprakarn Road. Tel: 716-801. Behind the Wang Come Hotel.

Shopping

Shopping is another prime reason visitors travel to Chiang Mai. Shops offer a wide selection of items and maintain handicraft workshops where you can watch the objects being made.

Antiques

Statues crafted from wood, bronze, terra cotta, and stone can be found in Chiang Mai's antique shops as can carved wooden angels, mythical animals, temple bargeboards, and eave brackets but you will find a better selection in Bangkok. Most items come from Burma, as the Thai government has banned the export of Thai Buddha images. Bronze deer, angels, and characters from the *Ramakhien* cast in bronze do not fall under the export ban. If you are interested in their decorative value rather than their antiquity, then consider neo-antiques.

Neo-Antiques

A sign on a shop 5km (3 miles) down H 108 says it all: 'Modern Antiques'. With genuine antiques in increasingly short supply, Thailand's artisans have turned to creating copies. There is no attempt to sell them as antique items and the craftsmanship is quite remarkable. Gods, animals, cute children, betelnut boxes and others in a variety of finishes are very popular. Shops also offer wooden furniture and can ship your purchases for you.

Baskets

Thailand makes some superb wicker and bamboo items but those found in Chiang Mai tend towards farm utensils. You can find lamps, storage boxes, tables, colourful mats, handbags, letter holders, tissue boxes and slippers in some of the larger emporia.

Banyen factory

Ceramics

Most Thai ceramics come from the North and best known among Chiang Mai's distinctive ceramics is celadon. The crazed jade-green glaze of this ceramics coats statues, lamps, ashtrays and other items. Pieces are also offered in dark green, brown and cobalt blue hues.

Modelled on its Chinese cousin, blue-and-white porcelain includes pots, lamp bases, household items and figurines. The quality varies widely depending on the skill employed and the firing and glazing.

Bencharong, (five colour pottery) describes a style of fine porcelain derived from Chinese art in the 16th century. Normally reserved for bowls and containers, its classic pattern surrounds small religious figures with intricate floral designs. The whole is rendered in five colours – usually green, blue, yellow, rose and black.

Earthenware includes a wide assortment of pots, planters, and dinner sets in a rainbow of colours and designs.

Decorative Items

Burmese in origin and style, *kalaga* wall hangings depicting gods, kings and mythical animals have gained immense popularity in the past few years. The figures are stuffed with *kapok* to make them stand out from the surface in bas relief.

Fabrics and Clothes

Bencharong porcelain

More than any other craft, Thai silk is synonymous with Thailand. Sold in a wide variety of colours, its hallmark is the tiny nubs which, like embossings, rise from its shimmering surface. Unlike sheer Indian silks, the thick, iridescent Thai

silk lends itself both to clothes and to use in decorative items for the house.

It is sold in plain or printed lengths or cut into scarves and other accessories. Tailors in Chiang Mai can fashion it into blouses and dresses but the quality of the cutting varies. If using a tailor, take along a magazine illustration or even an existing dress. Allow time for more than one fitting. You may be disappointed as tailors often visualise Thai bodies when cutting for *farang* figures.

Cotton is popular for shirts and dresses since it 'breathes' in the hot, humid air. Although available in lengths, it is generally tailored into frocks and shirts. In markets like Chang Khlan you can find hilltribe jackets, dark blue farmers' shirts and casual clothes.

Furniture

Wooden furniture can include cabinets, tables, dining room sets, bedroom sets or something as simple as a wooden tray or trivet. Chiang Mai specialises in carved floral and other motifs. It also offers a light whitewashed finish and pastel colours that transform a heavy piece of furniture into a decorative object.

Gems and Jewellery

Thailand is a leading producer of rubies and sapphires. Rough-cut and polished stones are sold for a fraction of their cost overseas. Artisans also craft jewellery to suit international tastes. Light green Burmese jade is carved into jewellery and art objects.

Be warned that there are unscrupulous dealers who pass off fakes as genuine and claim a gold content far in excess of the true value. Unless you know what you are doing, you can be cheated.

Ask for a certificate of authenticity but be prepared even then to have difficulty retrieving your money if you later discover the gem to be a fake.

Costume jewellery is a major Thai craft with numerous items available. A related craft which has grown popular in the past decade is that of gilding the orchids for which Thailand is justly famed.

Hilltribe Crafts

Hmong, Yao, Lisu, Lahu, Akha, Karen tribes produce a wide variety of brightly-coloured needlepoint work in geometric and floral patterns. Panels of these needlepoint work are sewed onto shirts, coats, bags and other clothing items.

Hilltribe silver work is valued less for its silver content (which is low) than for the intricate work and imagination that goes into making it. The selection includes necklaces, headdresses, bracelets and rings the women wear on ceremonial occasions.

Enhancing their value are the old British Indian rupee coins which decorate the women's elaborate headdresses.

Other hilltribe items include knives, baskets, pipes and a gourd flute that looks and sounds like a bagpipe.

Lacquerware

Lacquerware is a Lanna speciality and comes in two varieties: the gleaming gold and black type normally seen on the shutters of wat windows, and the matte red type with black and/or green details which originated in northern Thailand and Burma.

The lacquerware repertoire includes ornate containers and trays, wooden figurines, woven bamboo baskets and Burmese-inspired Buddhist manuscripts. The pieces may also be bejewelled with tiny glass mosaics and gilded ornaments.

Leather

The items are prosaic enough – shoes, bags, wallets, attaché cases, belts – but the animals which have contributed their hides are the oddest assortment: snake, armadillo, crocodile, cow hide stamped to look like crocodile, lizard, frog and even chicken.

Metal Art Objects

Although Thai craftsmen have produced some of Asia's most beautiful Buddha images, modern bronze sculpture tends to be of less exalted subjects and execution. Minor deities, characters from the classical literary saga, the *Ramakhien*, deer and abstract figures are cast up to 2m (6ft) tall and are normally annealed with brass, making them gleam. Bronze is also cast into handsome cutlery.

Silverworking is an ancient Chiang Mai art. Jewellery, trays and other handsome items are sold in the shops by the piece but in small home foundries are sold by weight. The craftsmanship can be extremely fine and the item can make a lasting gift.

Umbrellas

Perhaps Chiang Mai's most famous product, Chiang Mai umbrellas, once made from silk and oiled paper, now come in a wide variety of sizes and materials. Their beauty lies in the nature-inspired motifs hand-painted on them. No longer created simply to protect fair skins from the nasty sun, they can be as large as 4m (13ft) in diameter, big enough to shade a patio table.

Materials vary from cotton and silk to *sah* paper

made from pounded mulberry tree bark (a paper often called 'rice' paper), one of the oldest types of paper known. Huge silk fans used as wall decorations, and lampshades abound. Prices range from 15 baht for tiny umbrellas to 4,000 baht for the giants. Find a whole variety at Borsang Village, east of Chiang Mai.

Others

Nepalese and Tibetan: Thangkas, masks, turquoise jewellery, and other items are found along the eastern edge of Chang Khlan Road.

Personalized paintings: Chang Khlan Night Market artists paint flowers and your name on personal items like cigarette lighters, cameras and video cameras.

Puzzles: While away your time with a handmade wooden puzzle. There are at least a half dozen different types.

Pirated tape cassettes: At 25 baht they are so cheap you can buy them, listen to them and discard them when you leave.

Where To Shop

Shops along **Borsang Road** specialise in particular types of crafts. There are several large emporiums on the same road although they carrying slightly higher price tags and offering less chance to discover a treasure.

For **wood products**, drive through **Baan Tawai** south of Chiang Mai. The quality of carving and painting varies widely as do the types and finishes of items. Prices can be bargained and items can be shipped.

Hilltribe Productions Foundation: Operating under the patronage of King Bhumibol, the Foundation runs two shops. The main shop, Border Crafts of Thailand, is at 21/17 Suthep Road, Wat Suan Dok (Tel: 277-743) while the branch, Hilltribe Products Foundation (Tel: 212-978) is at 100/61-62 Huai Kaeo Road near Chiang Mai University. These shops; in a programme; run by the Royal Family, aid hilltribes in preserving their craft traditions and skills by providing them a market for their products. They are the only shops in town where the crafts of all the tribes can be found.

Bottoms up!

Silk fans

Calendar of Special Events

Plan your visit to coincide with a Thai festival. Thais celebrate their religious holidays with verve and invite the visitor to join in; do so. Dates change every year so it is advisable to check with the Tourism Authority of Thailand (TAT) first.

JANUARY

Borsang Umbrella Fair: This colourful festival honours the craftsmen of one of the oldest of Chiang Mai arts. There are competitions and exhibitions and the highlight of the fair is the selection of a Miss Borsang.

FEBRUARY

Luang Wiang Lakhon: Lampang's five most important Buddha images are paraded through the streets. Nightly Sound and Light presentation at the historic Wat Phra That Lampang Luang.

Flower Festival: Held when Chiang Mai's flowers are abloom. Flower exhibitions are staged but the key event is a grand floral procession through the streets of the city, with floats, marching bands and beautiful Chiang Mai women.

Makha Puja: Celebrates the spontaneous gathering of 1,250 disciples to hear Buddha preach. As the full moon rises, Buddhists gather at wats. Join in. Buy incense sticks, a candle and flowers from a vendor. After the chanting (40 minutes), follow the monk-led procession around the temple. After three circuits, place your candle, incense sticks and flowers in the sand-filled trays as others are doing, *wai* (hands clasped before the face) and depart.

APRIL

Poy Sang Long (Mae Hong Son only): Young Shan hilltribe men are initiated into the Buddhist monkhood in this ceremony.

Songkran: The traditional Thai New Year, finds the Thais at their boisterous best. One is supposed to bless his friends by sprinkling water on them, but it soon gets out of hand and water flies everywhere. Expect to get drenched and dress accordingly. The main action takes place on the banks of the Ping River.

MAY

Visakha Puja: Commemorates Buddha's birth, enlightenment and death, all of which occurred on the same day. Celebrated in the same manner as Makha Puja except that Chiang Mai residents walk up Doi Suthep to make merit.

Lychee Fair: Chiang Rai's lychee har-

vest is the reason for the celebration. The Lychee Fair features displays of agricultural products and handicrafts and a beauty contest to select a Miss Lychee.

Intakin Festival: Is held at Wat Chedi Luang for seven days and nights to invoke blessings for the city and its inhabitants.

JULY

Asalaha Puja: Commemorates Buddha's first sermon to his first five disciples. It is celebrated in the same manner as Makha Puja.

AUGUST

Longan Fair: Like Chiang Rai's Lychee Fair, Lamphun's Longan Fair celebrates the harvest of the fruit for which the town is best known: *lamyai*. Among the events is the selection of a Miss Lamyai, who joins the ranks of other northern beauty queens like Miss Garlic and Miss Onion.

SEPTEMBER

Chinese Moon Festival: Celebrated on the full moon night of the eighth lunar month. Do not miss the luscious moon cakes filled with nuts, durian, and salted eggs. Delicious.

NOVEMBER

Yi Peng Loy Krathong: Loy Krathong is the most beautiful of Thai celebrations. As the full moon is rising, Thais fill tiny floral boats with candles and incense and launch them into the rivers, canals, ponds, and the sea to wash away sins and bless love affairs.

It is a romantic night for lovers of all ages. Buy a *krathong* from a vendor, light the taper and incense, place in it a small coin and a few hairs plucked from your head, say a prayer and send it on its way down the Ping River. At nightfall there is a procession of prettily decorated floats down Tha Phae Road and past the Municipal offices. In recent years this festival has been ruined by excessive sale of fireworks. Take care of yourself – and of children.

Sunflower Fair (Mae Hong Son only): The Mexican Sunflowers are in bloom in the hills near Doi Mae U-Khor. Mae Hong Son organises a three-day festival of oxcarts decorated with the beautiful flowers. Cultural exhibitions, a beauty contest, film shows, music and a Thai Yai Folk Drama are also presented.

November through February: Buddhist temple fairs are held during the cool season to raise money for temple repairs. In the evening, villagers gather to enjoy local drama troupes, carnival rides, booths selling farm products. A convivial air of good fun.

DECEMBER

Chiang Mai Winter Fair (Chiang Mai only): The annual winter fair, held at the Municipal Stadium, offers cultural shows, the Miss Chiang Mai contest and a product fair.

Practical Information

GETTING THERE

By Air

Thai International operates a domestic service with comfortable planes.

There are fairly frequent daily flights between Chiang Mai and Bangkok. These flights take 60 minutes each way.

There are also daily flights to Chiang Rai, Mae Hong Son and Phitsanuloke. Phuket, Mae Sot and Tak are served by three or four flights each week.

Check details with the local office as flight schedules may change. Some flights may have Business Class seats at a small extra cost.

Flights to and from Mae Hong Son are liable to cancellation because of mist, rain or low cloud cover. Take this into account when planning your schedule.

By Rail

Each day, several train services run between Bangkok and Chiang Mai, covering a distance of 751km (467 miles). The day train journey takes 13 hours and requires lots of stamina but it is a more fun to travel.

Both the First and Second Class coaches are comfortable; sleepers are

available on these services. Food on the trains is not a problem as there is either a restaurant car and/or food vendors on board – not forgetting the station platforms.

The lazy journey to Chiang Mai can be a pleasant experience:

Shortly after leaving Bangkok it is dusk and time for something to eat and drink. By dawn the train is climbing slowly and the temperature is several degrees cooler. The tunnel at Khun Tan Station was built by Emil Eisenhofer in 1917. Then, the train descends and travels through rice fields and orchards until it reaches the terminus.

The trains can be very full at times and it is advisable to make advance reservations. There is a very efficient reservation office at Bangkok's Hualampong Station. Tickets can also be reserved at Chiang Mai Railway Station.

A Third Class ticket (for the adventurous) costs 275 baht, whilst a First Class ticket with sleeper costs about two times more – 555 baht. The Second Class tickets, with berths, are very popular.

However, these rates are likely to be increased in order for the trains to operate at a profit.

Day trains leave Bangkok's Hualampong Station daily at 6.35am and arrive in Chiang Mai at 8.05pm. Departure and arrival times are the same for the Chiang Mai–Bangkok day journey.

There are also three overnight

sleeper trains, the Nakhon Ping Express, which leave Bangkok at 3pm, 6pm and 7.40pm and arrive in Chiang Mai at 5.15am, 7am and 8am respectively.

The sit-up only Sprinter leaves Bangkok's Hualampong Station at 8.10am and arrives in Chiang Mai at 5pm, almost 15 hours later.

Bangkok–Chiang Mai day train

TRAVEL ESSENTIALS

When To Visit

The best months are mid-November through mid-February when the air is cool and the skies are clear. From February through May, the sun shines and it is cool and dry. The monsoon rain (June through mid-November) falls sporadically so that a visit can be pleasant albeit under frequently overcast skies.

During the Christmas and New Year holidays and the week of Chinese New Year facilities are strained to breaking point; book well in advance.

Visas and Passports

Royal Thai Embassies or Consulates around the world issue 60-day tourist visas for 300 baht. Permits to stay can be extended in Chiang Mai for an additional 30 days for a fee of 300 baht.

The same embassies also issue 30-day transit visas for 200 baht. They can be extended for another 30 days for a fee of 200 baht.

Most nationalities can obtain transit visas free on landing in Bangkok. These allow a stay of 15 days. Permission to extend can be obtained for a fee of 500 baht.

To extend your permit, go to the Chiang Mai branch of the Immigration Division (Tel: 277-510. Open Monday–Friday, from 8.30am–12pm and 1pm–4.30pm) of the Royal Thai Police Department, on the road approaching Chiang Mai Airport.

Take two passport-sized photographs and a photocopy of your passport. It normally takes about an hour to extend a permit.

Should you wish to stay in Thailand for more than 90 days, you must travel to Penang, Malaysia, Hong Kong, or Rangoon, and apply for a new visa. This normally takes two days. If you want to leave Thailand and return before your permit to stay expires, apply at the Chiang Mai Immigration office for a re-entry permit (500 baht) prior to your departure.

An exit visa is not required.

The Immigration Division enforces a strict dress code. Dress neatly and decently as visitors who are not wearing 'polite clothes' will not be served.

Vaccinations

Although the threat from cholera, polio and typhoid is minimal and inoculations are no longer required for entry into Thailand, vaccinations are recommended before you arrive. Smallpox is no longer a threat. If you arrive from a 'yellow fever area', you must have a certificate certifying recent inoculation.

Malaria is prevalent in the hills. The best medical advice is: Don't put your faith in anti-malarial pills. Avoid being bitten by mosquitoes. See a doctor and do not accept 'flu as a diagnosis if you develop a fever after you return from a trek. Insist on a blood test. Mention the possibility of malaria. Do not delay.

Money Matters

Thailand's principal currency unit the baht, is divided into 100 satang. Banknote denominations include a 1,000 (gray), 500 (purple), 100 (red), 50 (blue), 20 (green) and 10 (brown) notes.

Because the government is presently completing conversion from one set of coins to another, the coinage is confusing. There are two five-baht coins (silver with copper rims), two different one-baht coins (silver with copper rims), two 50-satang coins (brass) and two 25-satang coins (brass). Most public telephones now accept the smallest one-baht coin.

Thai currency is very stable and was rated at 25 baht to a US dollar at the time of publication. For daily rates, check the *Bangkok Post* or the *Nation* newspapers. Government rates are also posted at banks and exchange kiosks. There is no currency black market.

Hotels generally give poor rates, so change money at a bank. You will get better rates for travellers cheques than for cash.

Banks are open from 8.30am–3.30pm daily except Saturday, Sunday and bank holidays (when they could be closed for four days in a row). Banks also operate exchange kiosks all over Chiang Mai and Chiang Rai.

You can also use Visa and Mastercards to get cash advances up to your credit line at any of these banks: Bank of Ayudhaya, Thai Farmers Bank, Siam Commercial Bank and Thai Military Bank (see Useful Addresses).

Clothing

Clothing is casual; leave your suit at home. Natural fibres and blends are preferred because they breathe well in moist air. Cool season evenings can be quite chilly (the record low for Chiang Rai is 2°C (35°F). If trekking in the hills, it can be even colder. A sweater or woollen jacket will be welcome in the evenings or when travelling by motorcycle. Wear several layers of thin clothing that can be peeled off as the day warms.

Shorts and sleeveless blouses for men and women are frowned upon at Buddhist temples. Because shoes must be removed upon entering a temple, it is more convenient to wear sandals or slip-ons. Wear a sturdy pair of leather shoes or running shoes if you plan to motorcycle. A hat is advisable on a hot day as are sunglasses.

The winter months are surprisingly dry, so moisturising lotion and chapstick will be welcome, even in Chiang Mai. If travelling into remote areas, carry toilet paper, tampons, and towels. You will also want to carry a canteen of water; buy one along Manee Noparat Road.

Electricity

220 volts, 50 cycles. Electrical outlets take only flat-pronged plugs.

Airport Tax

The airport tax for passengers departing to other domestic destinations is 20 baht. A 200 baht tax for international flights is charged at the airport on departure.

GETTING ACQUAINTED

Geography

The North lies between Laos in the east and Tanen Taunggyi mountain range forming the Burmese border

A young Chiang Mai Miss

Time
Chiang Mai is +7 hours GMT.

How Not To Offend
Thais regard the Royal Family with genuine reverence. Avoid making slighting remarks about royalty and always stand when the Royal Anthem is played before a movie.

Show similar respect to Buddha images, temples and monks. Thais take a dim view of men or women wearing shorts and sleeveless dresses when visiting temples (it is amazing the number of cloddish visitors who, unthinkingly, wear sloppy or skimpy attire to holy sites).

Thais are reluctant to halt a sloppy foreigner so the obligation is upon you to respect their religion as you would your own. Remove your shoes when you enter a Buddhist temple or a Taoist shrine.

A monk's vow of chastity prohibits him from touching a woman, even his mother. Women should stay clear of monks to avoid accidentally brushing against them.

The Thai greeting and farewell is *Sawasdee*. It is uttered while raising the hands in a prayer-like gesture, the fingertips touching the nose, and the upper portion of the bodyslightly bowed forward. This gesture is called the *wai*. It is easy to master and will earn you smiles aplenty.

in the west; between Burma and the Mekong River in the north and upper rim of the Chao Phraya River Valley in the south. It is a hilly region with ranges running north and south and the towns occupying the valleys. In the North, Thailand's highest mountain, Doi Inthanon, towers 2,595m (8,514ft) above the surrounding hills.

Thailand's second largest city, Chiang Mai, is 600km (373 miles) north of Bangkok. It lies at the same latitude as Mexico City, Bombay, Timbuktu, and Hawaii whose climate its own resembles. Chiang Mai Valley is drained by the Ping River, one of four main tributaries which rise in the North and flow south to become the Chao Phya, the country's most important river.

Located in the geographic heart of the region, Chiang Mai is the North's undisputed capital. It sits 313m (1,027ft) above sea level, flanked by hills, including Doi Suthep, which rise to a height of 1,685m (5,528ft). Chiang Mai's population is more than 170,000.

Other key northern cities are Chiang Rai, Chiang Saen, Lampang, Lamphun, Nan, Mae Hong Son and Phayao. Most of the population live in villages. Two types of people inhabit the region: the Thais who are dominant, and a dozen hilltribes who are rice and vegetable farmers.

Thais believe in personal cleanliness. Even those dressed in poor clothes are neat and clean. They frown on unkempt and unbathed foreigners and may refuse them service or treat them with less kindness than if properly attired.

Thais believe that the head is the fount of wisdom and all parts of the body from there down are progressively unclean. It is, therefore, an insult to touch another person on the head, point one's foot at him, or step over him. Kicking in anger is worse than spitting at him.

Climate

The North's popularity stems in part from its pleasant climate. Temperatures between mid-November and January average between 13°C and 28°C (56°F and 83°F) in Chiang Mai; the hills are even colder than the city.

Temperatures begin rising in February and in the hot season (March–May) range between 17°C and 36°C (63°–97°F). In the rainy season (June–mid-November) the highs drop marginally but the lows, not at all. There is no considerable variation between day and night-time temperatures in any season.

The monsoon in the North begins (May) and ends (October) earlier than in Central Thailand. Overcast skies predominate but the rain generally falls sporadically except during September when an average of 250 mm (10 inches) crashes down and city streets often flood.

Tipping

Tipping is a new custom in Thailand, confined so far to large hotels and restaurants. Although a 10 percent service charge is added to the bill it usually goes to the owners so a small token to the waiter will be appreciated. In ordinary restaurants, tip no more than 10 percent. There is no tipping in noodle shops or street stalls. Room boys can be tipped but will not expect it. Transport drivers are not tipped.

Whom Do You Trust?

You may be approached by whispering Thais asking if you want drugs. While it is tempting to try them, be aware that the penalties for drugs are severe and that you may be set up for a drug bust after the peddler informs the police.

An even more sobering possibility is posed by the sign posted prominently at Daret's House restaurant:

'Stop and think.

If you think you are buying pure heroin, you could be wrong.

IT COULD COST YOU YOUR LIFE.

Six people were wrong this year. They're dead.

Drug pushers often inform the police.

Chiang Mai Jail – not nice.'

Tourist Information

The Tourism Authority of Thailand, the TAT, the Thai government's

Caption

official tourism promotion organization, maintains an office in Chiang Mai at 105/1 Chiang Mai-Lamphun Road on the eastern bank of the Ping River.

It offers numerous brochures on accommodation, travel agents, car rental and other services, besides promoting activities in Chiang Mai and other parts of the North. The office has friendly English-speaking officers who can answer most questions. Open from 8.30am–4.30pm. (Tel: 248-604, 248-607). On the ground floor is the office of the Tourist Police (Tel: 248-974).

Travel magazines are offered free at hotel reception desks. Although advertiser-oriented, they provide up-to-date information on current events. The English-language *Welcome to Chiang Mai* is the most comprehensive. It contains a great deal of background information, offers short features in French and Japanese, and has the best set of maps. *What's On, Where to Go* lists activities for the region.

GETTING AROUND

Airport To Town

At the southwest corner of the town, the airport is a 10-minute drive from city centre. Major hotel vans ferry guests with reservations (one can make a reservation at the airport) to their premises. They charge 100 baht per person.

Transport from Chiang Mai Airport into town (5km) consists of hotel courtesy cars and a limousine service which charges between 40 and 100 baht per person.

From town to the airport one can also travel by *tuk-tuk* or taxi. Call 277-318 for the limousine to collect you from your hotel.

Buses Around The City

Chiang Mai has two types of buses, the yellow and the red, plying five routes. Both charge two to four baht depending on the distance travelled.

Yellow

Route 1 runs east and west through the centre of Chiang Mai from the Superhighway to the base of Doi Suthep. It starts at the Superhighway, runs down Charoen Muang and Tha Phae Roads to Tha Phae Gate, turns left and follows the city wall, down Wua Lai and then north along Phrapoklao Road to the northern city wall, following it along Suthep Road past Wat Suan Dok and Wat U-mong to the Royal Project at the base of Doi Suthep.

Route 2 runs north and south, beginning at the Chang Pheuak Bus station, Phrapoklao Road, Rajawithi, Chang Moi, down the western bank of the Ping, through

the market, Chang Khlan, south on Charoen Prathet, crosses the Mengrai Bridge and finishes on the Chiang Mai-Lamphun Road.

Route 3 connects the railway station with the road up Doi Suthep. Beginning on Rat Uthit Road, it passes the station, crosses Charoen Muang Road and continues north

up Thung Hotel Road to Kaeo Nawarat Road, (the road to Doi Saket).

There, it turns left, crosses the Nakhon Ping Bridge, and then through the city on Chang Moi and Rajawithi Roads, Phrapoklao, and out to Huai Kaeo Road where you can catch a minibus to Doi Suthep.

Red

The red buses (un-numbered) circumambulate the town in opposite directions.

One bus takes this route: From the Chiang Mai Arcade Bus Station it travels south along the Superhighway for 4km (2½ miles) before turning right on to the circular road leading to the Airport. It then doubles back to the Airport Plaza intersection, turning left towards Suan Dok Gate and left again to the canal. Then, right into Huai Kaeo Road, right again as far as the Amari Rincome intersection and left onto the Superhighway, continuing round this circular route until it reaches its starting point.

The other bus route is in the opposite direction.

Taxis & Tuk-tuks

Tuk-tuks are motorised three-wheel taxis, so-named for the noise they make when running. Charges are according to distance and start at 10–20 baht. Bargain for lower rates before you board.

Samlors, the pedal trishaws, charge 10 baht for short distances. Bargain before you board.

Motorcycle taxis run up the Mae Sa Valley road from Mae Rim to Mae Sa Falls, passing the elephant camp and orchid farms.

Car Rentals

Cars and jeeps can be rented at several locations. You need a valid international driver's license or one from your home state. You have to surrender your passport for the duration of the rental period, so change money first.

Rates begin at 1,200 baht per day and mileage is unlimited: you pay for the petrol you use.

For example, Avis rents a Toyota Corona 1600 cc or Toyota Corolla 1300 cc/16 Valve for about 1,300–1,500 baht per day.

If you rent the car in Chiang Mai and leave it in Bangkok or another Hertz or Avis city, you must pay a drop fee of 2,500 baht.

When renting, read the fine print carefully and be aware that you are liable for all damage to the vehicle. Ask for a comprehensive insurance which covers you and other vehicles involved in a collision.

Avis: Main office: 14/14 Huai Kaeo Road. Tel: 222-013, 221-316. Open 8pm–5pm. Branches: Airport (Tel: 270-222) and Royal Princess Hotel (Tel: 281-033/034).

Hertz: Main office: 90 Sri Don Chai Road (Tel: 270-184/87) Branches: Chiang Mai Plaza Hotel

A mini bus

(Tel: 270-036) and Empress Hotel (Tel: 270-240).

Suda Car Rent: 18 Huai Kaeo Road. Tel: 210-030.

Aod Car Rent: 49 Chang Khlan Road, opposite the Night Bazaar. Tel: 279-197. Suzuki jeeps, cars, mini-buses with or without driver. Cars for rent from 500 baht and jeeps from 1,500 baht per day including insurance and unlimited mileage. You pay for fuel. Bargain if you are renting for several days.

Alternatively, you can hire a car with a driver to take you on day trips around Chiang Mai.

In front of major hotels, you can bargain with drivers to convey you anywhere in Chiang Mai and its environs for about 600 baht for an eight- or nine-hour day. He will wait for you at each site.

Drivers usually speak English and can often make suggestions of places to go. Avoid those offering to take you shopping; they will very likely collect a hefty commission from the shops they take you to.

Motorcycle Rentals

You must surrender your passport for the duration of the rental period so change money first. A photocopy may be accepted if you pay a deposit.

Motorcycles in Chiang Mai range from small 90 cc. Honda Dreams to 125 c.c. and 250 c.c. Honda, Suzuki and Yamaha trailbikes which have sufficient power to climb the North's

hills. Rental companies can be found along Chang Khlan Road, Tha Phae Gate, and Chaiyaphum Road.

Prices range from 150–500 baht/day. Rental is for a 24-hour period and you may be able to bargain the price down if you rent for several days. Unlimited mileage and you pay for your own fuel.

Bicycles

Shops along Chaiyaphum Road near Tha Phae Gate rent bicycles for 30 baht per day. The Galare Guest House and others also rent bicycles.

Maps

The best maps are included as part of a free monthly guide called *Welcome to Chiang Mai*. Each of the commercially produced maps is flawed in one way or another, usually in providing insufficient detail or imprecise locations.

A Pocket Guide for Motorcycle Touring in North Thailand by David Unkovich is a guide book rather than a map, but it is the only accurate survey of the roads and touring conditions in North Thailand. It contains 23 strip maps, each accurate and very simple to use.

P&P 89 Promotions produces *Tourist Map of Chiang Mai, Rose of the North* which has a very good map of the North but its map of Chiang Mai is not detailed enough and its bus route notation is virtually impossible to decipher. Still, it is the best of the commercial maps.

The *Tourist Map of Chiang Mai*

Bicycles for rent

An indication of rates charged during the high season is given by referring to the following codes for rates per night (taxes included):

$ = less than 500 baht
$$ = between 500–1,000 baht
$$$ = between 1,000–2,000 baht
$$$$ = between 2,000–5,000 baht
$$$$$ = over 5,000 baht

During peak holiday periods (holidays, Christmas, New Year, etc), accommodation is at a premium rate. But for the rest of the year, it is always worth asking for a discount – Remember, you won't get one if you don't ask!).

If you are calling the hotel or guesthouses from outside the regions below, please note that the telephone area code for the regions covered below is 053.

Chiang Mai

(See also Mae Rim)

published by the TAT may cause a bit of confusion since the city map is exactly the same as the P&P 89 Promotions map and is equally unhelpful. What it does contain is a series of regional maps of the north with the names of places in both Thai and English.

D.K.'s Tourist Map offers street maps of Chiang Mai, Chiang Rai, Mae Hong Son. It is very sloppy in its placement of each location with Samoeng placed in the wrong location). The map also lacks an overview of the North.

Like her popular *Bangkok Market Map*, Nancy Chandler's colourful *Chiang Mai Market Map* is a detailed guide to the bargain shopping spots of the city and a mine of minutia that make shopping fun.

CHIANG INN
100 Chang Khlan Road.
Tel: 270-070/071.
Bangkok office: 251-6883.
170 rooms. $$$

CHIANG MAI ORCHID
100 Huai Kaeo Road.
Tel: 222-091/99.
Bangkok office: 233-8261.
267 rooms. $$$$

CHIANG MAI PLAZA
92 Sri Don Chai Road.
Tel: 270-036/50.
Bangkok office: 253-1276.
444 rooms. $$$$

DIAMOND RIVERSIDE
33/10 Charoen Prathet Road.
Tel: 270-299, 270-080.
300 rooms. $$$

ACCOMMODATION

Hotels

The following is a selection of hotels from among the many available. They have been chosen to show a range of facilities and prices available and, in a few cases, because they are different.

Note that accommodation tariffs can change without advance notice. Hotels also charge a value added tax (VAT) of 7% and a service charge at 10% or more.

Novotel Suriwongse
110 Chang Khlan Road.
Tel: 270-051.
Bangkok office: 251-9883.
168 rooms. $$$

Pornping
46-48 Chareon Prathet Road.
Tel: 270-110/17.
325 rooms. $$$

Quality Chiangmai Hills
18 Huai Kaeo Road.
Tel: 210-030/34.
Bangkok office: 260-0050.
281 rooms. $$$

Royal Princess
112 Chang Khlan Road.
Tel: 281-033/034.
Bangkok office 233-1130 ext. 2874.
198 rooms. $$$$

River View Lodge
25 Charoen Prathet Road, Soi 4.
Tel: 271-110.
36 rooms. $$$

The Empress
199 Chang Khlan Road.
Tel: 270-240. Fax: 272467.
375 rooms. $$$

Guesthouses

Daret's House
4/5 Chaiyaphum Road.
Tel: 235-440.
28 rooms. $

Galare
7/1 Charoen Prathet Road.
Tel: 273-885.
35 rooms. $$

Je t'Aime
247-9 Chareon Rat Road.
Tel: 241-942.
24 rooms. $

Top North
15 Moonmuang Road.
Tel: 278-684.
63 rooms. $

Chiang Rai

Dusit Island Resort
129 Kraisorasit Road.
Tel: 715-777.
288 rooms. $$

Wiang Inn
893 Paholyothin Road.
Tel: 711-543.
260 rooms. $$

Wang Come
869/90 Premwiphat Road.
Tel: 711-800.
221 rooms. $$

Golden Triangle G.H.
590 Paholyothin Road.
Tel: 711-339.
9 rooms. $$

Mae Kok Villa
445 Singhalai Road.
Tel: 711-786.
44 rooms. $

Chiang Dao

Chiang Dao Hills Resort
KM 100 Chiang Mai-Fang Highway.
Tel: (in Chiang Mai) 236-995, 232-434. Bangkok office: 225-0551. $$

PIANGDAO
Soi 1, Main Highway
10 rooms. $

Chiang Saen

THE GOLDEN TRIANGLE RESORT
222 Golden Triangle.
Tel: 714-031.
75 rooms. $$$

CHIANG SAEN G.H.
45 Tambon Wiang.
18 rooms. $

Fang

CHIK THANI HOTEL
425 Mu 5 Chotana.
Tel: 451-252.
60 rooms. $$

Mae Hong Son

HOLIDAY INN MAE HONG SON
Khunlumpraphat Road.
Tel: 611-231.
114 rooms. $$$

TARA MAE HONG SON
149 Mu 8 Tambol Pang Mu.
Tel: 611-483.
104 rooms. $$$

PIYA COMPLEX
1 Soi 3, Khunlumpraphat Road.
Tel: 611-260. $

Pai

CHARLIE'S HOUSE
5, Rungsiyanon Road.
Tel: 699-039.
Located next door to Krungthai Bank on Rungsiyanon Road. Accomodation here is clean, comfortable and, more importantly, safe.

Mae Sarieng

MIT AREE G.H.
34 Wiang Mai Road.
Tel: 681-109.
67 rooms. $

Mae Rim

ERAWAN RESORT
30 Moo 2.
Tel: 297-078.
59 rooms. $$

MAE SA RESORT
KM 3 Mae Rim-Samoeng Road.
No telephone. $

MAE SA VALLEY
86 Mu 2, Mae Sa.
Tel: 297-980. $

Mae Sai

MAE SAI
125/5 Paholyothin Road.
Tel: 731-462.
50 rooms. $

Tha Thon

THIP'S TRAVELLERS HOUSE
Next to the bridge over Kok River.
Tel: 245-538. $

MAEKOK RIVER LODGE
On the Kok river, near the bridge.
Tel: 215-366.

BUSINESS HOURS

Banks are open daily from 8.30am to 3.30pm except Saturday, Sunday and bank holidays. Exchange kiosks are open 8.30am to 8.30pm. Post offices are open Monday to Friday from 8.30am to noon and from 1pm to 4.30pm. The Central Post Office near the railway station is open on Saturday mornings. The Airport Post Office is open every day of the year from 8.30am to 8pm. Businesses are open the usual office hours, except for hairdressers and barbers which tend to close on Wednesday. Shops suit themselves.

PUBLIC HOLIDAYS

The following days are observed as official public holidays.

New Year's Day: 1 January.
Makha Puja: February/March, during the full moon.
Chakri Memorial Day: 6 April.
Songkran: 13 April.
Labour Day: 1 May.
Coronation Day: 5 May.
Ploughing Ceremony: In May.
Visakha Puja: May/June, during the full moon.
Asalaha Puja: July/August, during the full moon.
H.M. the Queen's Birthday: 12 August.
Chulalongkorn Day: 23 October.
H.M. the King's Birthday: 5 December.
Constitution Day: 10 December.
New Year's Eve: 31 December.
Chinese New Year: January/February, is not officially recognised as a holiday but many shops are closed, often for several days.

HEALTH AND EMERGENCIES

Hygiene
Drink bottled water or soft drinks and save tap water for bathing and teeth-brushing. Most hotels and large restaurants offer bottled water and clean ice. Mineral water is both cheap and easily available from roadside stalls or supermarkets. Thai chefs understand the importance of hygiene and the chances of becoming ill from food poisoning are minimal.

With its thriving nightlife and transient population, Thailand is a magnet for venereal disease. Protect yourself. AIDS on the rise, so there is even more reason to be careful.

Pharmaceuticals are produced to international standards and pharmacies are required to have registered pharmacists on the premises. Most pharmacy personnel in the shopping and business areas speak English.

Health Precautions
Motorcycle accidents account for the majority of tourist injuries in Chiang Mai. So take extreme care. Do wear a helmet, proper shoes and long pants when riding.

Malaria has not been eradicated in the hills of the North and the occasional case still surfaces, especially during the rainy season. In most major populated areas, you will not have a problem.

Take ample precautions, nevertheless, and use repellent and a mosquito net to prevent yourself from being bitten. Do not place your faith on anti-malarial pills. If you develop a fever on returning from a hill trek, consult a doctor immediately and insist on a blood test. Suggest the possibility of malaria.

Rabies. The incidence of rabies is not high, but you should still take immediate action if you are bitten by a dog.

Wipe off the saliva from the wounds and wash thoroughly under a running tap or with plenty of water for at least five minutes, using soap or detergent. Apply an antiseptic (but do not use cetrimide).

Note the description of the dog and its owner, if any. If it has an owner or can be kept under restraint, ask somebody to keep it under observation for the next 10 days. If the dog is still alive after 10 days, it is not rabid. But if it dies, it should be taken to a hospital laboratory to determine whether it died of rabies or some other cause.

Immediately after being bitten, consult a doctor who is an orthodox practitioner of western medicine. Insist on starting the full course of six injections immediately. This is crucial if the bite is on the head or neck, especially for children.

The injections should be administered on the day of the being bitten, and on days 3, 7, 14, 30 and 90 after that.If the dog is still alive on the 10th day after the bite, the last three injections may be remitted.

Hospitals
Chiang Mai

LANNA HOSPITAL
Off the Superhighway on the north-east side of town.
Tel: 211-037/41.

CHIANGMAI RAM HOSPITAL
8/4 Boonrueng Rit Road (near Sri Tokyo Hotel).
Tel: 234-787.

SUAN DOK HOSPITAL
Corner of Boonruangrit and Suthep roads across from Wat Suan Dok.
Tel: 221-122.

Chiang Rai

CHIANG RAI PRACHURUKHRO HOSPITAL
Sathanpayaban Road.
Tel: 711-300.

Lamphun

LAMPHUN HOSPITAL
Chamathewi Road.
Tel: 511-034.

Mae Hong Son

SRISONGWAN HOSPITAL
Srihanat Bamrung Road.
Tel: 611-378.

Medical clinics
Chiang Mai

LOI KROA CLINIC
62/2 Loi Kroh Road.
Tel: 271-571.
Monday–Friday 7.30am–1pm, 4.30pm–8.30pm. Saturday mornings and Sunday evenings.

CHANG PHEUAK POLYCLINIC
52/2 Chang Pheuak Road.
Tel: 210-213.
Weekdays 7am–8am, 5pm–9pm; weekends 8am–9pm.

CHATAWAT POLYCLINIC
100/11-12 Huai Kaeo Road.
Tel: 216-222.
Daily 9am–2pm, 5pm–9pm. Specialises in dermatology.

Chiang Rai

CHIANG RAI CLINIC
234 Thanalai Road.
Tel: 711-234.

Dentists
Chiang Mai

SEVENTH DAY ADVENTIST DENTAL CLINIC
228/4-5 Doi Saket Road
Tel: 491-813.
Sunday to Thursday.

โรงพยาบาลปาย
PAI HOSPITAL

DR KITTI CLINIC
2/3 Ratchawong Road.
Tel: 234-787.
5pm–8pm.

DR. SOMCHAI DENTAL CENTER
131 Kotchasan Road.
Tel: 252-939, 234-423.
Offers 24-hour dental services.

Note: All the dental clinics listed above are located in Chiang Mai. Call first to make an appointment.

POLICE EMERGENCIES

Theft

A special Tourist Police force assists travellers with inquiries or recovery of stolen goods. Its office is on the ground floor of the Tourism Authority of Thailand office on the Chiang Mai-Lamphun Road. Tel: 248-974.

Most Tourist Police officers can speak English.

Long Distance Bus Rides

There are new warnings from the police against accepting drinks or sweets from strangers.

Several years ago, a number of tourists on trains and buses were drugged and robbed. Police put a stop to the practice but it seems to have arisen again.

This is a sad development because Thais are naturally generous and accepting an offer of food can be the beginning of a great friendship.

The best advice is to judge the giver and if you have any doubts about him, politely refuse the gift.

Credit Card Fraud

For several years there have been problems in some of the guesthouses with tourists leaving their credit cards in the safety deposit boxes while they went on a hilltribe trek. The cards were returned to them but when the credit card company bills arrived, there were numerous items charged on a shopping spree while the owner was in the hills.

It is probably best if you leave home without it; if it is stolen in the hills (see below) you will not very likely have time to inform card company authorities until you get back to Chiang Mai.

In general, exercise caution when using credit cards. Last year, 40 percent of all American Express credit card fraud worldwide occurred in Thailand. Ask for and destroy your carbons and if someone has to take the card elsewhere to check your credit line, go with him.

Hilltribe Treks

The incidence of armed robberies of trekkers has declined but there are still occasional problems.

The perpetrators are hilltribesmen or, very often, employees of rival trekking companies trying to discredit popular firms. Carry what you need and no more.

A special police force for tourists

COMMUNICATIONS & NEWS

Postal Services

The Central Post Office (Tel: 246-541/4; open Saturday mornings only) is at Charoen Muang Road,

A post-box

near the railway station). Post offices are open Monday–Friday, 8.30am–noon and 1pm–4.30pm. There are a number of sub-post offices round the town, a useful one is on Prasani Road on the north side of Tha Phae Road, before reaching Nawarat Bridge. The post office at the airport is open daily from 8.30am to 8pm.

The Tourism Authority of Thailand (TAT) in Chiang Mai also offers a mail and message service where friends can send you letters. Get them to address the letters to you, care of:

TOURISM AUTHORITY OF THAILAND
105/1 Chiang Mai-Lamphun Road
Chiang Mai 50000

Telephones & Fax

Large hotels provide long-distance telephone and fax services. There is also a long-distance service at the General Post Office and at private shops along Chang Khlan and other streets in Chiang Mai. Some booths charge a base three minutes for overseas calls. Fax services are also available on request.

To call abroad directly, first dial the international access code 001, followed by the country code: Australia (61); France (33); Germany (49); Italy (39); Japan (81); Netherlands (31); Spain (34); UK (44); US and Canada (1).

If you are using a US credit phone card, dial the company's access number. Sprint, Tel: 001 99913 877; AT&T, Tel: 001 999 1 1111; MCI, Tel: 001 999 1 2001.

Shipping

Shops will generally ship for you but if you have bought items at a number of shops and want to ship them your-

self, go to the Central Post Office which sells special cardboard shipping cartons. A half a dozen shops nearby will also box and wrap packages for you. If you have a big shipment, utilise the services of these shipping companies:

BOONMA MOVING
24/1 Soi 5, Nantaram Road.
Tel: 274-467.

CHIANG MAI AIR CARGO
234/2 Wua Lai Road.
Tel: 271-655/56.

HONG KONG INTERNATIONAL MOVERS
13/7-8 Moo 1, Sankampaeng Road.
Tel: 246-951.

News Media

Thailand's English daily newspapers, the **Bangkok Post** and the **Nation** are available in Chiang Mai before 11am each day. Both newspapers are morning papers

Hotels and shops also offer British, German and French newspapers but they are expensive.

Radio

Chiang Mai University broadcasts news and cultural programs in English. Daily 6am–8.30am and 6pm–10pm on 96.5 MHz FM. Light music is also broadcast daily on 100.8 MHz FM.

110

Bookshops

SURIWONG BOOK CENTRE
54/1-5 Sri Donchai Road.
Tel: 281052-5.

D.K. BOOK HOUSE
244-40 Tha Phae Road.
Tel: 235-151.
Possibly the best collection of books, magazines, newspapers, guide books and maps in Chiang Mai.

ANTIQUES – EXPORT PERMITS

The Fine Arts Department prohibits the export of all Buddha images and of images of other deities and fragments (hands or heads) of images dating from before the 18th century.

If you purchase one, the shop can register it for you. Otherwise, you must take it to the Fine Arts Department in Bangkok on Na Prathat Road across from Sanam Luang, together with two postcard-sized photos of it. Export fees range from 50 to 200 baht, depending on the antiquity of the piece.

Fake antiques do not require export permits but Thai Airport Customs officials are not art experts and may mistake it for a genuine piece. If it looks authentic, clear it at the Fine Arts Department to avoid problems later.

FURTHER READING

History
An Asian Arcady, Reginald Le May. White Lotus, Bangkok. 1986. This is an excellent account of the history of the North in the early years of the century. Originally published in 1926, Foreword by Major Roy Hudson FRAS.

A Short History, David K.Wyatt.

Yale University Press, Thailand. 1982. There are few good histories of Thailand and none on the history of Chiang Mai. This is the best of what there is, with references to Chiang Mai and its relations with surrounding countries.

Hilltribes
Lanna Textiles, Patricia Cheesman and Songsak Prangwatthanakun. Suriwongs Book Centre, Chiang Mai. 1987. A superb study of many of the woven fabrics found in Lanna.

A Life Apart, Jon Boyes and S. Piraban. Suriwong Book Centre, Chiang Mai. 1989. A series of 23 fascinating interviews with members of six hilltribes about their lives, customs and perceptions.

A Trekkers Guide to the Hilltribes of Northern Thailand, John R. Davies. Footloose Books, Wiltshire, U.K. 1989. A good overview of the northern hilltribes and their customs.

Peoples of the Golden Triangle, Paul and Elaine Lewis. Thames and

Hudson, London. 1984. An excellent consideration of six hilltribes by a missionary couple who spent their lives working among them.

Drug Trade

The Politics of Heroin in Southeast Asia, Alfred W. McCoy. Harper and Row, New York. 1972. A compulsively detailed study of the heroin trade in the region but particularly in the Golden Triangle. Reprinted in 1989.

Travel

Insight Guide: Thailand and *Insight Pocket Guide: Thailand*, Apa Publications. Both have sections on Chiang Mai and northern Thailand.

Consul in Paradise, W.A.R. Wood. Souvenir Press, London. First published in 1965. Reprinted in 1991. The memoirs of a cheerful Englishman who arrived in Chiang Mai as a translator in 1908 and ultimately became the British Consul.

De Mortuis. The Story of the Chiang Mai Foreign Cemetery, R.W. Wood. Chiang Mai, 1992, 4th edition. A collection of some 70 biographical sketches of pioneer missionaries, timber company employees, diplomats and others who lived and died in the north and who are buried or commemorated in the Chiang Mai Foreign Cemetery. (established 1898). Written by a long time resident of Chiang Mai who knew very many of them and whose father lived in Chiang Mai 100 years ago. Available from the cemetery caretaker on Chiang Mai-Lamphun Road or from D.K. Book House or Suriwong Book Centre.

Teak-Wallah, Reginald Campbell.

Oxford University Press, Singapore. 1986. The memoirs of an Englishman working in Thailand's forests in the 1920s. The book was written at a time when it never occurred to anyone that one day the hills could be denuded of their trees.

Temples and Elephants, Carl Bock Oxford University Press, Singapore. 1986. The memoirs of a Norwegian traveller and naturalist. Originally published in 1883.

A Thousand Miles on an Elephant in the Shan States, Holt Hallet. White Lotus, Bangkok. 1988. First published in 1890. An entertaining and valuable piece of work.

SPORTS

Exercise

Chiang Mai has two fitness parks. **Huai Kaeo Fitness Park** is the older and more attractive of the two. It is wedged between the Arboretum and the Zoo on Huai Kaeo Road. The other is on the Suthep end of Nimanhaemin Road. Both are open from 5am–10pm.

Golf

Lanna Golf Course on Chotana Road.(Tel: 221-911) has 18 holes. Daily 6am–6pm. Green fees on weekdays: 400 baht; weekends: 600 baht. Caddy: 130 baht. Clubs rental: 200 baht.

Gymkhana Club Golf Course, Rat Uthit Road off the Chiang Mai-Lamphun Road. A nine-hole course on the grounds of the city's oldest private club. Green fees, weekdays: 300 baht; weekends: 400 baht. Caddy: 100 baht. Clubs available for rent from 300 baht. Tel: 241-035 for reservations.

Hot Putt

The **Green Valley Golf Club** has an 18-hole course. It is on the right-hand side on reaching district town of Mae Rim. Green fees on weekdays: 1,000 baht; weekends 1,500 baht; (lower during low season). Caddy: 150 baht. Tel: 297-426.

Chiang Mai Golf Driving Range, 239/3 Wua Lai Road. Tel: 282-838. Open 7am–10pm. Charges: 25 baht per bucket of balls.

Hash House Harriers

The Harriers were founded by British soldiers in Malaysia as a means of making running fun.

The 'Hares' string a paper trail through the back-country, laying down as many false clues as they do true ones. The 'Hounds' follow the trail through marshes, canals and rice fields to reach the goal: frosty bottles of beer.

The Chiang Mai branch departs from the Black Cat Bar on Moon Muang Road every second Monday at 4pm. Telephone Tony at 216-793 for more information.

Horse Riding

Lanna Horse Riding Club: Located near race course on Mae Rim Road, the club charges riding fees of 250 baht per hour. Saddles, etc, provided. Helmets for hire. Tel: 217-956 .

Jogging

Thais begin at the bottom of Doi Suthep and jog to the top. If you think this too strenuous, jog through Buak Hat City Park in the southwest corner of the city, just inside the city wall.

Snooker

Plaza Snooker Club, located on the First Floor of the Chiang Mai Plaza Hotel. Open 11am–1.30am. Charge: 100 baht/hour.

Squash

Gymkhana Club, Chiang Mai-Lamphun Road. Tel: 241-035. Daily 7am–8pm. Rackets can be hired.

Tennis

If the **Rincome Hotel courts** are not being used by guests, they can be rented by outsiders.

Otherwise, go to **Anantasiri Court**, 90/1 Superhighway (opposite Chiang Mai Museum). Tel: 222-210. Daily 7am–7pm except Tuesdays. You can rent tennis rackets, balls and hire an instructor for coaching sessions here.

A game of Tennis

Windsurfing

Lake windsurfing is available at Huai Tung Tao, **Agricultural Development Centre** (Chotana Road, enroute to Mae Rim). Board rental: 100 baht/hour. Go there on a windy day and try your luck.

SPECIAL INFORMATION

Thai dates

The traditional Thai dating system found on many old buildings accords to the birthdate of the Buddha in 543 BC. (called BE or Buddhist Era). Thus, to arrive at the Roman date, subtract 543 from the number i.e. BE 1867 - 543 = 1324.

Glossary of temple terms

Bot. A wat ordination hall, usually open only to the monks. A *bot* is identified by six *bai sema* or boundary stones around the outside of the building which define the limits of its sanctuary. Many *wats* do not have *bots*, only *viharns*.

Chedi. Often interchangeable with stupa. A spire surmounts a mound in which relics of the Buddha or revered religious teachers are kept.

Chofah. The bird-like decoration on the ends of a *bot* or *viharn* roofs.

Galae. The 'horns' at the peak of a Lanna house.

Ku. A square, normally gilded,

Windsurfing at the Agricultural Development Centre Lake

brick and stucco structure in the middle of a northern *viharn* that houses a Buddha image.

Naga. A mythical serpent, usually found slithering down the edge of the roof. In sculpture, it shelters Buddha as he meditates.

Sala. An open-sided pavilion.

Viharn. The sermon hall; the busiest building in a *wat*. A *wat* may have more than one.

Wat. Translated as 'temple' or 'monastery' but describing a collection of buildings and monuments within a courtyard wall.

The Thai language

The short phrase list given below has been transcribed into a Romanized form in accordance with the General System for Romanization of Thai Characters into Roman, as notified by the Royal Institute in 1954.

This system is meant for general use and for spelling geographical names. It does not make use of diacrtiical marks to indicate tones or length of vowels.

However, as Thai has five tones and short and long vowels I have inserted in the following phrase list diacritical marks as shown below:

Tones: High ^ Low ˘ Falling ˋ Rising ´
There is also a middle tone for which there is no diacritical mark.

Vowels. All single vowels have a short sound. All underscored vowels or diphthongs have a long sound.

Consonants. Give these their pure values as for English consonants, except for 'kh', 'ph' and 'th' which have a small but definite release of breath after the k, p or t sound.

Ask an English-speaking Thai friend to pronounce the words '*pai*' (meaning 'to go') and '*phai*' (meaning 'to paddle'), you may hear the difference in pronunciation.

Note also that 'ph' is NOT pronounced like 'f' in photo, nor is 'th' soft as in 'thigh'.

Polite particles. The word *khrap* is a polite particle used by men at the end of most sentences. By itself it means 'Yes'. Women use the word *khă* which changes to *khâ* at the end of questions.

First person pronoun. The safe word for 'I' for men is *phom*, whilst women should use *dichan* or its diminutive *chan*.

Questions. To ask a question, add the word *mái* at the end of the phrase. For eg, *rao pai* (meaning 'We go') becomes *rao pai mái* (Shall we go?).
To negate a statement, insert the word *mài* between the subject and the verb, eg., *rao mài pai* (We shall not go).

A word of warning. Thais living in the seven northern provices speak a language amongst themselves known as *kham muang*, or the language of the country. This is quite different from Bangkok Thai.

These days, though, nearly all speak Bangkok Thai and casual visitors trying out their language skills will have enough on their hands with the phrases shown below.

Visitors would do well to forget about learning *kham muang* in addition to Bangkok Thai.

English	Thai

Numbers

One	*nŭng*
Two	*sóng*
Three	*sám*
Four	*sí*
Five	*hà*
Six	*hŏk*
Seven	*chĕt*
Eight	*pǎet*
Nine	*kào*
Ten	*sĭp*
Eleven	*sĭp ĕt*
Twelve	*sĭp sóng*
Thirteen	*sĭp sám*
Twenty	*yì sĭp*
Thirty	*sám sĭp*
100	*nŭng rôi*
1,000	*nŭng phan*

Days of the Week

Monday	*wan chan*
Tuesday	*wan angkhan*
Wednesday	*wan phût*
Thursday	*wan phâreûhăt*
Friday	*wan sŭk*
Saturday	*wan sáo*
Sunday	*wan arthît*
Today	*wan nî*
Yesterday	*menu wan nî*
Tomorrow	*phrŭng nî*
When?	*mua rai*

Greetings and others

Hello	*sawătdi*
Goodbye	*la kon*
How are you	*sabai di réu*
Well, thank you	*sabai di khráp* (or *khà*)
Thank you very much	*khŏp khun màk*
May I take a photo	*khó thăi rùp nŏi*
Never mind	*mai pen rai*

I cannot speak Thai	*phóm (chán) phùt thai mài dài*
I can speak a little	*phóm (chán) phùt dai nît nŏi*
Where do you live?	*khun yŭ thì nái*
What is this called in Thai?	*nî phásá thai riàk wá arai*
How much?	*thào rai*

Directions and Travel

Go	*pai*
Come	*ma*
Where?	*thì nái*
Right	*khwá*
Left	*sâi*
Turn	*liêo*
Straight ahead	*trong pai*
Please slow down	*khâp châ châ noi*
Stop here	*yŭt thì nì*
Fast	*reo*
Hotel	*rong raem*
Street	*thanón*
Lane	*soi*
Bridge	*saphan*
Police Station	*sathăni tamruàt*
Market	*talat*

Hill words

Hill	*doi*
Mountain	*phu kháo*
Trail	*thang doen pă*
Tree	*tòn maî*
Village	*mŭ bàn*
This way	*thang nî*

Useful phrases

Yes	*khráp (khà)*
No	*mài*
Good	*di*
bad	*mài di*
Do you have…?	*…mi mái*
Expensive	*phaeng*
Very expensive	*phaeng màk*

Do you have something cheaper?	mi thŭk kwa nî mái
Can you lower the price a bit?	lôt dài mài
Do you have another colour?	mi sí eŭn mái
Too big	yăi koen pai
Too small	lêk koen pai
Do you have anything larger?	mi yăi kwă nî mái
Do you have anything smaller?	mi lêk kwă nî mái
Where is the toilet?	suàm yŭ nái khrâp (khâ)

Other handy words

Hot (heat)	akăt rôn
Hot (spicy)	phêt
Cold (weather)	akăt náo
Cold (object)	yĕn
Sweet	wán
Sour	priào
Delicious	aroi

USEFUL ADDRESSES

Banks
Chiang Rai

BANGKOK BANK
53-9 Tha Phae Road.
Tel: 233-454.

BANK OF ASIA
149/1-3 Chang Khlan Road.
Tel: 270-029.

BANK OF AYUDHAYA
222-6 Tha Phae Road.
Tel: 236-509.

SIAM COMMERCIAL BANK
17 Tha Phae Road (Entrance round the corner on Chang Khlan Road).
Tel: 276-122.

THAI FARMERS BANK
169-71 Tha Phae Road.
Tel: 270-157.

Mae Hong Son

BANGKOK BANK
68 Khunlumpraphat Road.
Tel: 611-546.

THAI FARMERS BANK
76 Khunlumpraphat Road.
Tel: 611-556.

Chiang Rai

BANGKOK BANK
517 Suksathit Road.
Tel: (053) 711-248.

SIAM COMMERCIAL BANK
552 Tanalai Road.
Tel: 711-515.

THAI FARMERS BANK
537 Bupprakarn Road.
Tel: 711-515.

Airline Offices

THAI INTERNATIONAL
(international and domestic)

CHIANG MAI
240 Phrapoklao Road.
Reservations: 210-043, 211-044.
TG Airport Counter: 270-222.

CHIANG RAI
870 Paholyothin Road.
Tel: 711-179, 713-863.
Airport: 711-464.

MAE HONG SON
71 Singhanathamrung Road.
Tel: (053) 611-297, 611-194.
Airport: 611-367.

ART/PHOTO CREDITS

Photography	
Front cover, 6, 7, 10, 11, 65, 69, 85	**Luca Invernizzi Tettoni**
Back cover	**Steve Van Beek**
18, 20, 33, 34, 39, 41, 44, 50, 55, 80, 83	
94, 95, 98, 105, 106, 107, 114	**Ingo Jezierski**
92	**Jean-Leo Dugast**
93	**Dallas and John Heaton**
Update Editor	**Roy Hudson**
Maps	**Berndtson & Berndtson**
Cover Design	**Klaus Geisler**

INSIGHT GUIDES

COLORSET NUMBERS

You'll find the colorset number on the spine of each Insight Guide.

INSIGHT *pocket* GUIDES

• •
United States: Houghton Mifflin Company, Boston MA 02108
Tel: (800) 2253362 Fax: (800) 4589501

Canada: Thomas Allen & Son, 390 Steelcase Road East
Markham, Ontario L3R 1G2
Tel: (416) 4759126 Fax: (416) 4756747

Great Britain: GeoCenter UK, Hampshire RG22 4BJ
Tel: (256) 817987 Fax: (256) 817988

Worldwide: Höfer Communications Singapore 2262
Tel: (65) 8612755 Fax: (65) 8616438

66 I was first drawn to the Insight Guides by the excellent "Nepal" volume. I can think of no book which so effectively captures the essence of a country. Out of these pages leaped the Nepal I know – the captivating charm of a people and their culture. I've since discovered and enjoyed the entire Insight Guide Series. Each volume deals with a country or city in the same sensitive depth, which is nowhere more evident than in the superb photography. 99

Sir Edmund Hillary

NOTES